PRAISE FOR *SUST*

. . . .

"Do you long to recover the art of discipleship in your church or ministry? If so, Walt Russell's *Sustainable Church* is a must-read. Russell has given the Church a gift in *Sustainable Church*—a practical manual for building a congregation rather than an organization. If you long to be preoccupied with disciples rather than dollars, this book is for you. If you seek to align more with the New Testament than with corporate strategy, these pages will refresh and reinvigorate you."

JOHN S. DICKERSON
AUTHOR OF *THE GREAT EVANGELICAL RECESSION*

"If you want to read a remarkable scholar of the New Testament and spiritual growth, if you want insights on evangelism and the vitality of the people of God, if you want to live out the Great Commission through the local church in a more biblical way, read what Walt Russell has to say in *Sustainable Church*. Walt is as wise as he is knowledgeable. I know that first hand, and my leadership has been strengthened through his words and his life."

BARRY COREY, PH.D.
PRESIDENT OF BIOLA UNIVERSITY

"Walt Russell has devoted his life to understanding the call Christians have to be the church. Even more so, Walt has dedicated himself to embracing Christ's call to be a sustainable and organic body of believers that grows deep as the whole body ministers together. We have both known Walt as teacher and mentor, and we trust he will serve you as a helpful guide to the Bible's calling to follow Christ."

JAMIN GOGGIN AND KYLE STROBEL
AUTHORS OF *THE WAY OF THE DRAGON OR THE WAY OF THE LAMB: SEARCHING FOR JESUS' PATH OF POWER IN A CHURCH THAT HAS ABANDONED IT*

"For too long the church has imported corporate leadership models from the business world and confused them for sound ecclesiology. The result is an inorganic, cumbersome, top-down system prone to fall quickly apart when one leader leaves or another gets burnt out. In *Sustainable Church*, Walt Russell presents a compelling case for the better (and more biblical) model, one that is bottom up, nimble, and organic. At a time when the local church in western culture is facing new social, theological, and economic pressures, a sustainable model is more needed than ever. Anyone who cares about a thriving local church should read and share this book!"

BRETT MCCRACKEN
AUTHOR OF *HIPSTER CHRISTIANITY* AND *GRAY MATTERS*

"Walt Russell's *Sustainable Church* is a must-read for thinking Christians who care about the future of the church. I found it so very refreshing to encounter a work on ecclesiology that is deeply rooted in Scripture, rather than in the latest trends in secular leadership or church growth. I came away from Walt's book at once both heartbroken and hopeful. I was heartbroken, as I reflected upon the myriads of saints who have never experienced their calling as gifted servants of Christ—all because of the institutional orientation of a big-box Christianity that relies on the gifts of a few to nurture a passive consumerism on the part of the many. I was hopeful, as well, however, because Walt's book brought me back—through a careful examination of the Scriptures—to a biblical model of local church life that involves everyone in the joy of ministry. *Sustainable Church* is both prophetic and educational. It may not be well received by those who are deeply invested in the ecclesiastical status quo. So be it. Those who have ears to hear, however, will find in *Sustainable Church* one of the most meaningful and biblically sound treatments of local church life and ministry available today."

JOE HELLERMAN
AUTHOR OF *WHEN THE CHURCH WAS A FAMILY*

"Walt Russell has been a faithful and diligent follower of Christ for many years. We have had the honor of witnessing his genuine joy in Christ as well as his tears of spiritual conviction about God's desires for the body of Christ. Walt's understanding and careful applications of the Scriptures to his life, and especially to the church, have qualified him to be a clear, reliable, and compassionate teacher to all who would seek to embody the teachings of Jesus and His apostles. Do you find it ironic, as we do, that so many who take the New Testament seriously in various theological matters have somehow conveniently overlooked the plain, but revolutionary New Testament teaching, implications, and practices of what Walt has termed the "organic" and "sustainable" forms of being/doing church? *Sustainable Church* is a timely clarion call to reform and renew wisely the way we think about and engage in being Christ's Church. We intend to take Walt's empowering insights and loving challenges to heart as we depend on the Spirit's grace and power to serve our local church community well and the other church families and movements to whom He sends us."

MICHAEL AND TERRI SULLIVANT
FOUNDERS OF RADIUS MINISTRIES AND NEW HOPE COMMUNITY OF KANSAS CITY
MICHAEL IS AUTHOR OF *PROPHETIC ETIQUETTE*

"*'Why haven't we heard this before?'* is a question you will ask many times as you read Walt Russell's much-needed book. The sustainable church is organic rather that institutional, where members minister to each other by using their "grace gifts" instead of relying on leaders to do the work. The sustainable church is where disciples are formed in nurturing communities rather than through individual effort. The sustainable church is, well, sustainable. And it's not just the church of the future. *It's church we need right now.*"

STAN JANTZ
BESTSELLING AUTHOR AND EXECUTIVE DIRECTOR OF
EVANGELICAL CHRISTIAN PUBLISHERS ASSOCIATION

SUSTAINABLE CHURCH

Growing Ministry Around the Sheep,
Not Just the Shepherds

WALT RUSSELL, PH.D.

First Edition

Cover design and layout by Rafael Polendo (polendo.net)

Some of the anecdotal illustrations in this book are true to life and are included with the permission of the persons involved. All other illustrations are composites of real situations, and any resemblance to people living or dead is coincidental.

Unless otherwise identified, all Scripture quotations in this publication are taken from the *New American Standard Bible*®, Copyright © 1960, 1962, 1963, 1968, 1971, 1972, 1973, 1975, 1977, 1995 by The Lockman Foundation. Used by permission. www.lockman.org. Scripture quotations marked "ESV" are from the ESV Bible® (The Holy Bible, *English Standard Version*®), copyright © 2001 by Crossway Bibles, a publishing ministry of Good News Publishers. Used by permission. All rights reserved. www.crossway.org. Scripture quotations marked "NIV" are taken from the Holy Bible, *New International Version*®, NIV®. Copyright © 1973, 1978, 1984 by Biblica, Inc.™ Used by permission of Zondervan. All rights reserved worldwide. www.zondervan.com

ISBN 978-0-9913345-8-2

This volume is printed on acid free paper and meets ANSI Z39.48 standards.

Printed in the United States of America

 QUOIR

Published by Quoir
Orange, California

www.quoir.com

DEDICATION

....

Dedicated to my profoundly beautiful, spiritual, and encouraging wife, Marty, for her unfailing love of me and her faithful partnering in the work of Christ over our forty-two and a half years of marriage. I love you!

TABLE OF CONTENTS

....

PREFACE

. . . .

"The prudent see danger and take refuge, but the simple keep going and suffer for it."

–Proverbs 27:12
(NIV)

"The American church stands today in a similar position, on the precipice of a great evangelical recession. While we focus on a few large churches and dynamic national leaders, the church's overall numbers are shrinking. Its primary fuel—donations—is drying up and disappearing. And its political fervor is dividing the movement from within. In addition to these internal crises, the outside host culture is quietly but quickly turning antagonistic and hostile toward evangelicals."

–John S. Dickerson
The Great Evangelical Recession

"We evangelicals have failed to pass on to our young people an orthodox form of faith that can take root and survive the secular onslaught. Ironically, the billions of dollars we've spent on youth ministers, Christian music, publishing, and media has produced a culture of young Christians who know next to nothing about their own faith except how they feel about it. Our young people have deep beliefs about the culture war, but do not know why they should obey scripture, the essentials of theology, or the experience of spiritual discipline and community. Coming generations of Christians are going to be monumentally ignorant and unprepared for culture-wide pressure."

–**Michael Spencer**
"The Coming Evangelical Collapse"
(Christian Science Monitor)

"'There is certainly a growing trend towards bi-vocational ministry in both mainline and evangelical churches,' says Kurt Fredrickson, a professor of pastoral ministry at Fuller Theological Seminary in Pasadena, California. This trend dovetails with other recent developments that are troubling to many religious communities. Not only is church attendance in long-term decline, but financial giving by church members is at Depression-era lows. Meanwhile, seminary students are taking on ballooning debt for a career that may not exist by the time they graduate. This trend began before the Great Recession, and has only worsened since then."

–**David R. Wheeler**
"Higher Calling, Lower Wages"
(The Atlantic)

MUSINGS ON A CRICKET BASKET

....

Five years ago my wife Marty and I visited northern Louisiana and stayed in a lovely house on a lake. The owners of the home knew that I liked to fish and they graciously gifted us with a bait basket full of crickets. Fishing with crickets was relatively new to me, so after my first morning of fishing, I was intrigued to observe the cricket bait container and its now-depleted population.

The first thing I noticed was that if the crickets had just looked straight up, they would have been able to jump or crawl up and through *the huge opening* in the top of the basket. However, they seemed content to settle for the confines of the familiar. They could see the outside world through the fine mesh walls of the basket, but they could not join it. Apparently, seeing it was enough. I did notice that a very small percentage of crickets had jumped or crawled out of the container by the next morning, but the vast majority was still captive and crawling up and down the same walls, over and over. Their immediate goal seemed to be avoiding the big hand that periodically invaded their space.

Christians can be a bit like the crickets in the cricket basket. We have had our familiar containers—church traditions—for many centuries. Many aspects of these traditions restrict us in a confined space, where too often we are satisfied to remain. We *climb the walls* and crawl over and over the same limited terrain. We are captive to our traditions, our containers, rather than creatively living outside these familiar boundaries.

Not that I am against traditions. I am not. But, like Jesus, I am against tradition when it supersedes the Word of God (Mark 7:8).

More specifically, I am against those traditions that trap Christians in shallow, pragmatic, unsustainable containers that suck the organic life out of God's people. These human-crafted traditions go back over 1900 years. They are very old, very revered, and very familiar containers. We have Catholic baskets, various Orthodox ones, many Protestant types, and shiny evangelical versions of every shape and color. However, the common feature of almost all these unsustainable, non-organic containers is that *they keep us from experiencing the rich, organic, life of the church.* They do this by making the focal point of our containers the priest-like ministry of our leaders. They do this by creating the expectation that we must stay in the container and keep focused on these leaders. For heaven's sake, *don't look up.* Don't jump or crawl up to freedom, to a life that demands unceasing creativity so that the organism of the church might flourish in a sustained manner in her mission. Rather, we end up building *an artificial life—a non-organic life*—around our leaders in our container-communities and then wait and watch out for the big hand that periodically grabs at us.

This book is about our life-in-community *outside of* those restrictive church containers. It is a book that challenges us to look up and be willing to jump or crawl through the big opening that God's Word presents. It is a book about reimagining what our life together in Christ should look like as we see it taught and modeled in the New Testament. It is about "the sustainable church" that God designed.

My primary goal is not to disparage our present churches, although there is much that is disturbing in our history. Rather, my purpose is to call the church to build her ministry sustainably around the sheep, rather than unsustainably around the shepherds. I'll seek to sketch the picture that the New Testament gives of this type of church—a church intended to be an amazing *organism* with an astonishing sustainability in every culture throughout the world. My hope is that you will have the courage and interest to look up and leap into embracing this life.

This is my prayer for you, dear reader, as you read this book:

"Now may the God of peace who brought again
from the dead our Lord Jesus,

the Great Shepherd of the sheep,

by the blood of the eternal covenant,

equip you with everything good that you may do His will,

working in *us* that which is pleasing in His sight
through Jesus the Messiah,

to Whom be glory forever and ever. Amen."

(Hebrews 13:20-21)

Chapter One

OUR SHALLOWNESS MAKES US UNSUSTAINABLE

....

Americans are a very pragmatic people. Our efficiency may be our greatest strength, but also our greatest weakness. So let's begin to answer the question, "Why is the shallow American church not sustainable over the long haul?" with a very pragmatic argument. Let's take a look at *First Evangelical Non-Organic Church.*

FIRST EVANGELICAL NON-ORGANIC CHURCH

Over the course of the last month, this church of 200 adults has encountered the following issues with its members and regular attendees:

1. A young family with sick kids has some big medical bills that are swamping their monthly budget.

2. Coming for some counsel at the encouragement of concerned friends in the youth group is a teenager who has been dabbling in the Goth culture at her high school.

3. His "Bible as Literature" class causes a college student who grew up in the church to come back home on spring break

with lots of questions and gnawing doubts about the Christian faith.

4. On the brink of losing their home, a financially troubled family with over $40,000 in credit card debt comes and seeks advice.

5. A young wife whose husband is on active duty with the military in the Middle East confesses that she has developed an emotional relationship with a co-worker.

These sorts of issues can be multiplied all over the country in countless evangelical churches. They are the problems of everyday life in America. But how does the non-organic church—the traditional way we do church—meet these everyday needs of God's people?

Here's how First Evangelical Non-Organic Church responded to the needs mentioned above:

1. The young family with sick kids and big medical bills got referred to the pastor who referred them to one of the deacons, who promised to bring up their situation at next month's deacons' meeting discussion of the Benevolence Fund. Six weeks later the beleaguered family received a $100 check in the mail and a note explaining that the Benevolence Fund was depleted because of the recent economic downturn.

2. Since the church was in between youth pastors again, the interim couple leading the high school group referred the teenager with a growing interest in Goth culture to the semi-retired pastor in charge of the church's Care and Community Ministry. He was very sorry that he couldn't be of much help when he met

with her because he really didn't know anything about the values and beliefs of Goth subcultures.

3. Having just returned from a conference on how to become a mega-church, the executive pastor was able to meet with the university student with growing doubts about the Christian faith. The frazzled, slightly jet-lagged pastor promised to send the student some helpful information. He eventually had his secretary photocopy some pages out of one of his seminary textbooks, mailing them to the student with a short explanatory note.

4. The financially-troubled family with over $40,000 in debt met once with the pastor, who referred them to a local debt-counseling center. They received solid advice on how to restructure their finances. Nevertheless, they felt very sad about the plan to eliminate their giving to the Lord for the next five years while they paid off their credit card debt.

5. The young wife who was having an emotional affair with a co-worker met with the pastor and he referred her to the semi-retired pastor in charge of Care and Community. This older pastor was very fatherly and gracious with her, but did not feel qualified to help her walk through the situation. He referred her to a professional counselor in the area who proved to be very helpful. However, the cost became prohibitive for her after a few weeks and she had to quit. She soon resumed the destructive relationship with her co-worker.

FLAWS IN MEETING NEEDS *WITHIN* THE NON-ORGANIC CHURCH

Please let me make one thing very clear. I am not criticizing pastors for *not* being omnicompetent, omnicaring, and omnipresent. Having been a pastor for many years, I observed that many pastors are overworked, underpaid and under-loved. But that is precisely the problem. Our traditional way of doing church, grounded in some long-held but unbiblical ideas,[1] is not working. From the examples above, we note two fundamental flaws:

1. The paid professionals are assumed to be omnicompetent and therefore skilled and capable to meet the vast array of issues and needs that arises in the parade of human concerns. They cannot possibly fulfill such unrealistic expectations. Moreover, they are expected to direct a cumbersome, institutional structure that can be astonishingly slow in addressing immediate needs. Herein lies one key flaw of the non-organic church: We default to our *organizational structures* to minister to others rather than function out of *the organic structure* of the body of Christ.

2. Additionally, "the clergy" are almost always viewed as the primary gatekeepers and permission-givers for any meaningful ministry that occurs in the life of the non-organic church. There may be some short-term efficiency in such a design, in certain situations. More often it results in needs getting lost in the structural bureaucracy of the church. While gatekeepers can be helpful, permission-givers usually are not. Requiring permission before people can use their gifts and minister to others thwarts the organic functioning of the

body of Christ. *Organization* should not triumph over *organism.*

Thinking along these lines undermines biblical teaching, falsely defining *ministry* as something that *professional ministers do.* Our language condemns us on this point. The ministers are "clergy" and the rest of us—the unwashed masses—are "the laity." As the old joke goes, "They are paid to do good and the rest of us are good-for-nothing!"

FLAWS IN PERSUADING THOSE *OUTSIDE* THE NON-ORGANIC CHURCH

The non-organic church is clunky in meeting the needs of God's people *within the church.* But it also fails to persuade those *outside the church* of the truth of the gospel.

In response to the growing secularization of culture, many American Christians have been gripped by the fear of losing a prominent place for Christianity in society. To counter the growing secularization, however, we have wrongly turned to *exercising political power* rather than focusing on being a redemptive, organic community: "It is not an exaggeration to say that *the dominant public witness of the Christian churches in America since the early 1980s has been a political witness."* [2]

Our focus on cultivating political power rather than vibrant, organic Christian community has led us off track in mission. I would add my voice to James Davison Hunter's in a prophetic call for the church to stop talking about "redeeming the culture," "transforming the culture," "advancing the kingdom," and "changing the world" because such talk implies *conquest and domination.* This approach and the biblical and cultural presuppositions that undergird it are problematic. As Hunter pointedly says, "This account is almost wholly mistaken."[3]

Rather, the church should incarnate God's word of love in *faithful presence*, as God's people have done at numerous times throughout church history. As Hunter asserts, we need to emphasize "faithful presence" and develop "a post-political witness" while not abandoning our distinctiveness:

> The desire to be *defensive against* the world is rooted in a desire to retain distinctiveness, but this has been manifested in ways that are, on the one hand, aggressive and confrontational, and on the other, culturally trivial and inconsequential. And the desire to be *pure from* the world entails a withdrawal from active presence in huge areas of social life. In contrast to these paradigms, the desire for *faithful presence* in the world calls on the entire laity, in all vocations—ordinary and extraordinary, "common" and rarefied—to enact the shalom of God in the world.[4]

Hunter's appeal to the mobilization and ministry of all of God's people—unfortunately called *laity* (I hate that word!)—is how we get out of the quagmire. Imagine how creative God's people could be in showcasing the truth and beauty of the gospel if they are released to minister and equipped to use their grace-gifts in their vocations, neighborhoods, and everyday settings. The "strategy" to influence the culture would not be any strategy at all, but rather the organic expression of the body of Christ as it lovingly ministers in a myriad of individual and communal ways to a needy world.

CONCLUSION

There are fundamental flaws with the non-organic church. Our basic template is more informed by ecclesiastical tradition, political strategizing and American success principles than by Scripture. We need to shed our shallow and unsustainable habits. We need to change because our traditional way of doing church does not work. It does not work in meeting the needs of those *within the church* because it puts the burden (and responsibility) entirely on paid ministers and fails to mobilize everyone else who Jesus gifted to minister. It also does not work in meeting the needs of those *outside the church* who desperately need to be persuaded to believe in Jesus Christ. It fails because the truth and beauty of the gospel is lost amidst the bureaucracies and polemics of the non-organic church. There must be a better way to go. We must stop oiling the machinery of the shallow, unsustainable church and start tilling the fertile soil of the organic sustainable church. We must focus on growing the saints' ministry and not just the senior pastor's. We must build our ministry around the sheep, *not* the shepherds. This is our only hope for meaningful sustainability.

Chapter Two

WE THWART THE GROWTH OF THE CHURCH'S ORGANIC PARTS

....

"In the beginning, the church was a fellowship of men and women centered on the living Christ. Then the church moved to Greece, where it became a philosophy. Then it moved to Rome, where it became an institution. Next it moved to Europe where it became a culture, and, finally, it moved to America where it became an enterprise."

–Dr. Richard C. Halverson[1]

The non-organic church—our traditional way of doing church—stands in stark contrast to the analogy of the church as a living organism—a body. The Apostle Paul makes this analogy in several passages in four of his epistles: Romans, 1 Corinthians, Ephesians and Colossians.[2] His point in these passages is that the church has a *unity*, crafted by the Holy Spirit under Christ's headship, that is similar to the unity or oneness of the human body: "so we, who are many, are *one body* in Christ, and individually members of one another" (Rom. 12:5; my emphasis).[3]

Coupled with this Spirit-crafted unity of the body of Christ is *an astonishing diversity* of members (body parts) that fuel the unity, the growth and the sustainability of the body/church: "from whom *the whole body, being fitted and held together by what every joint supplies,*

according to the proper working of each individual part, causes the
growth of the body for the building up of itself in love (Eph. 4:16;
my emphasis).[4]

THE TRAGEDY OF A NON-FUNCTIONAL BODY

What can the body of Christ do if the vast majority of its body
parts—members—are constrained and non-functioning? What
would a human body look like if many of the parts of the cir-
culatory and respiratory system, the digestive system, the endo-
crine system, the excretory system, the nervous system, the skel-
etal system and the reproductive system were not functioning?
What if many of the 206 bones, or 650-850 muscles, or over one
billion nerves in an adult human body were not functioning? It
would likely take *a very small percentage* of non-functioning parts
to kill a human body.

But what if I had several non-functioning parts in my body
and was still alive? What if I had paralyzed arms, legs, and hands?
What If I had poor blood circulation and trouble breathing?
What if I also had such serious digestive problems that I had to
have my colon removed? What if I had no sight, smell, or sound
due to non-functioning eyes, nose, and ears? You get the picture.

When you saw me in my wheelchair, you would surely have
great sorrow for me in light of the quality-of-life losses that my
inert body was experiencing. You would likely also have great
indignation at the under-performance of my body in light of
a normal body's amazing capabilities. You would hopefully be
aghast at the tragedy of a body with so many parts failing to
function as they were created to function.

Why don't we have similar feelings of sorrow, indignation
and horror when we see a *spiritual* body with the vast majority
of its parts failing to function as they were created to function?

26

We have intense emotions viewing an under-performing human body created to function on earth for 70 to 90 years, yet we feel very little when we see the under-performing body of Christ—an entity designed to function *for the rest of eternity.* What's wrong with this picture?

How non-functioning and unsustainable is the body of Christ? We have not broadly measured the percentage of Christians who know what their grace-gifts are and are fully functional members of the body. However one study in 2009 by the Barna Group did explore the spiritual gifts that Christians say they have.[5] Here are a few of the findings:

- 68% of Christians say they have heard of spiritual gifts (compared to 71% in 1995 and 72% in 2000; we're going the wrong direction).

- 21% of the "spiritual gifts" claimed by the respondents included *non-biblical gifts* like a sense of humor, singing, health, life, happiness, patience, a job, a house, compromise, premonition, creativity and even clairvoyance!

- 63% of those surveyed who have heard of spiritual gifts have not been able to apply this information to their lives because they either don't know their gift (15%), say they don't have a spiritual gift (28%) or claim that spiritual gifts *are not biblical* (20%)

These amazing findings raise very significant questions about *what* the 68% of Christians who have heard about grace-gifts actually heard. This is deeply disturbing data.

I recently led a seminar with a men's group in a large evangelical church in Southern California. I asked them, "What percentage of the body of Christ in the United States that is evangelical is functioning because these believers know and are using their grace-gifts?" Do you know what they said? *5-10%*. I'm going to be very magnanimous and estimate a figure closer to 20%, though it would surprise me if more than *one in five* evangelical Christians knows what his or her organic role (body part) is in the body of Christ. The reality is probably closer to *one in ten*.

Moreover, *being functional* in one's grace-gifts is not just about knowing which ones *you want to have*. Rather, *being functional* is working with the assigned organic roles that *you do have*: "But now God has placed the members, each one of them, in the body, just as He desired" (1 Cor. 12:18). It is essential that we believers discover where we have been crafted by Christ via the Holy Spirit to fit within His organism—the body of Christ. It is essential that certain leaders within the body help us find our role. We'll talk more about this in Chapters Five and Thirteen.

In the absence of leaders focusing on equipping the saints to function healthily in their Christ-given organic role, we end up with a minimally mobilized, under-performing spiritual body and overworked paid professionals. We end up with a body where 80-90% of its members/parts are *non-functioning*. This is the ugly reality of churches like Chapter One's First Evangelical Non-Organic Church. The paid professionals are supposed to be both omnicompetent—which they are not—and the permission-givers for all meaningful ministry to others. Nothing could be further from the biblical picture of a fully functioning, organic body of Christ.

BADLY NEEDED EXERCISE

In many ways the present condition of the non-organic church is very much like how Bud Wilkinson, the legendary Oklahoma University football coach, described professional football: "A professional football game is a happening where 50,000 spectators, desperately needing exercise, sit in the stands watching 22 men on the field desperately needing rest."[6]

Such is the body of Christ as many in today churches understand it. The vast majority of the saints, desperately in need of spiritual exercise, sit with folded hands and watch the paid professionals, who are desperately in need of rest. I fear that we run the risk of our loving Savior assessing the handiwork of *our tradition of doing church* and saying to us what He said to the Pharisees: "And by this you invalidated the Word of God for the sake of your tradition." (Matt. 15:6b; Mark 7:13).

CONCLUSION

The bottom line—a good business term—is that we are thwarting the growth of most of our organic parts—God's people—and thereby wasting their contribution to our organic growth. We are wasting the grace gifts that Messiah Jesus has given to us. We are wasting the precious time that He has given to each of us to use our gifts. We are wasting the growth that would occur if the organism that is the body of Christ were fully functional. God is sovereign in all of this, but *we* are accountable. This is why we must nurture the sustainable church by equipping the vast majority of her members—the saints—to do the work of ministry. We desperately need the functioning of the other 90-95% of our organic body parts, "from whom *the whole body, being fitted and held together by what every joint supplies, according to the proper working of each individual part, causes the growth of the body for the building up of itself in love*" (Eph. 4:16; my emphasis).

Chapter Three

GLIMPSING THE SUSTAINABLE CHURCH

....

"The whole of the church is greater than the sum of her parts." It sounds like this might be a profound statement, but what in the world does it mean? It means this: When we saints from the non-organic church are nurtured and equipped to discover and fulfill our organic role in the body of Christ through the use of our grace gifts, our impact in sustainable, organic community with fellow believers is far greater than the impact each of us could have individually.

This chapter envisions how rich and profound the ministry of the saints can be when we are equipped to use our gifts in community with one another. We quite seamlessly become *the sustainable church* because we become a healthy local body that reproduces itself in other healthy, local bodies. *Being sustainable* is not about becoming larger. It is about being organically healthy and reproductive.

Any human body part is only effective when it functions in organic harmony with its fellow body parts. So it is in the body of Christ. We should express our grace gifts *in submission to* Messiah Jesus' authority and in *organic* community *with* our fellow brothers and sisters in Christ. I cannot emphasize enough the phrases *in submission to* and *in organic community with*. The body of Christ is an organism that has a head—Jesus—and an organic, *family-like* structure. Look at this body from every conceivable angle and you will see that it runs on relational ball bearings. If we cannot get along with Jesus or with our fellow body members, we bring absolute chaos and devastation to the organism. This is because the body of Christ is *not* fundamentally about authority, but relationships. We will speak more about this later. But for the moment let me give you a proof of the centrality of relationships in the use of our grace gifts. It is a glimpse of the saints growing outside of the non-organic church as they are nurtured to grow in their organic ministry as the people of God.

A BODY THAT LOVES LOVE

1 Corinthians 12-14 is the longest discussion of grace-gifts in the New Testament. Right in the middle of this discussion is chapter 13, which is about the fact that I could have any (or all) of the grace gifts and could use them with great expertise, and yet if I "do not have love, I am nothing" (1 Cor. 13:1-2). Moreover, "if I give all my possessions to feed the poor, and if I surrender my body to be burned, but do not have love, it profits me nothing" (13:3).

   Love is the preeminent priority.

   While the grace gifts will cease and pass away, "love never ends" (13:8 ESV). These gifts are wonderfully important to the ministry and edification of God's people, but they are for *now*—this present age. They will cease when this age and the church are completed or perfected at the return of Messiah Jesus (13:10).[1] Contrasted to *now* is *then*—when we shall have full, not partial knowledge (13:9-10); when we will have mature, not childish thoughts and communication (13:11); and when we shall know God "face to face" and will know more fully (13:12).

All of Paul's reasoning points to the absolute necessity for using grace gifts in a relationally-loving manner. The grace-gifts will not cross over to the age-to-come. However, *all the love expressed through using our grace-gifts* will pass over because love has an unending essence, not a temporary one like grace gifts (13:8). This astonishing relational dimension should undergird and permeate all of our discussions and expressions of grace gifts. Like it or not, the body of Christ rolls on organic, family-like, relational ball bearings that incarnate and showcase God's love for humanity in Christ. This is an absolutely essential characteristic of the sustainable church.

LAST EVANGELICAL ORGANIC CHURCH

To drive this point home, let's return to problems that First Evangelical Non-Organic Church was having in Chapter One, but address them with an alternative set of responses that flows more from the organic nature of the body of Christ pictured in the New Testament. These organic responses *flow from saints who have been nurtured to minister and equipped to fulfill their God-given role in the body of Christ.* These responses are not found in First Evangelical Non-Organic Church, but in Last Evangelical Organic Church.

1. A young family with sick kids has some big medical bills that are swamping their monthly budget.

When this word travels through the body of Last Organic Church, it immediately stirs the hearts of members of the body with grace gifts that will help meet these needs. First on the scene are usually those with the gift of mercy (Rom. 12:8).[2] These dear saints understand about how to do the harder part of Romans 12:15: "Rejoice with those who rejoice, and weep with those who weep." Their first order of business is to connect emotionally with this vulnerable young family's pain of financial anxiety.

Next, they seek to help alleviate the financial pressure by letting the body know about this young family's needs. Of course, this is done *formally* in the assembly—the official church gathering—during the time set aside for "body life." However, it is also done *informally* through the church's organic web of interpersonal relationships. Given the immediacy and vibrancy of the relational network, news of this family's needs quickly falls on the ears of at least two saints with the gift of giving (Rom. 12:8). Following Jesus' instructions, they *anonymously* give to the needy young family so that the left hand does not know what the right hand is doing (Matt. 6:3). Within two or three days, the emotional and financial needs of this young family are met by the organic expression of the Spirit-gifted saints who have been nurtured and equipped to function in community with their fellow believers. Through compassionate giving the body builds itself up in love.

2. Coming for some counsel at the encouragement of concerned friends in the youth group is a teenager who has been dabbling in the Goth culture at her high school.

The diversity of the grace gifting of the body of Christ is astonishing. So it is not the least bit unusual within the diversely gifted saints of Last Organic to find a saint like Gina with the gift of the distinguishing between spirits (1 Cor. 12:10). In light of her gifting, Gina is very skillful in distinguishing the difference between spirits of truth and error. Her grace gifting helps her to embody the Apostle John's exhortation to "test the spirits to see whether they are from God" (1 John 4:1-6).

At the encouragement of the elders, Gina has been reading voraciously about the various kinds of spiritual deception in

American culture. She has been particularly concerned about the recent growth of neo-paganism in our society, of which parts of the Goth culture are expressions. Out of these concerns she starts to lead a small group study focusing on the issue with interested members of the youth group. Therefore, when one of the group's members observes this teenager hanging out with the Goth group at high school, he contacts Gina, who sets up a time to meet her after school. Over coffee Gina spiritually discerns the teenager's level of involvement, then helps to educate and warn her about the malevolent spiritual power behind certain Goth beliefs. After a couple of meetings, the teenager becomes wiser and more spiritually discerning about the reality of spiritual warfare. She also expresses a greater love of Jesus because she realizes that His triumph over the spirit world is a crucial part of her salvation in Him (Col. 2:8-15). Being loved by such concerned and thoughtful Christians also gives the vulnerable girl a sense of belonging and security that she had not felt before. Gina's Spirit-given sensitivity to spiritual counterfeits protected this young believer who, in turn, was motivated to find her own unique place among the equipped saints at Last Organic. This is yet another way the grace gifts enable the body to build itself up in love.

3. His "Bible as Literature" class causes a college student who grew up in the church to come back home on spring break with lots of questions and gnawing doubts about the Christian faith.

One of the beautiful aspects of equipping the saints to minister is that a very high percentage of them discover their grace gifts, grow in their use of them, and are *intrinsically motivated* to minister using their gifts. Bob is one of the many saints like this at Last Organic. He makes his living as a mechanical engineer and as an occasional adjunct math professor at the local community college. However, his avocation and passion is reading in the area of apologetics—defending the faith. He is particularly excited about sharing what he learned at a recent "Defending the Faith Conference" at Biola University.[3] The elders had heard about this conference, asked Bob to go to it, and the church covered the cost. When the saints at Last Organic are earnest and faithful in the use of their gifts, the leaders take note. They understand that a vital part of shepherding the flock is aggressively *initiating* the ongoing equipping of the saints.

Bob is motivated by the Holy Spirit to study apologetics because he has the grace gifts of evangelism (Eph. 4:11) and teaching (1 Cor. 12:28-29; Rom. 12:7). These gifts, in conjunction with his personality and vocational training, give him a strong internal motivation to explain and defend the Christian faith. He delights in sharing what he is learning with his colleagues and students at the community college. When he hears of the questioning college student, he leaps at the opportunity to talk to him about his doubts. Doing a little more research on the Internet and in his own library of apologetics books, this saint is more than ready to walk with the student through his key issues and to put some very helpful reading material in his hands. It is an incredible relief to this student to know that there are good answers to his questions and that there are equipped saints in the body who can eloquently express these answers. He is also challenged by Bob to mature as a Christian so that he is "always being ready to make *a defense* [Greek, *apologia*] to everyone who asks you to give an account for the hope that is in you" (1 Peter 3:15b). He now has a vision of how he too can become a vital, functioning part of the community of equipped saints at Last Organic.

4. On the brink of losing their home, a financially troubled family with over \$40,000 in credit card debt comes and seeks advice.

We have been blessed in recent years to see God raise up several evangelical ministries that teach people how to handle their finances.[4] These wonderful ministries have made their materials and training readily accessible to local churches. The result is that there are saints in many congregations who have been equipped in this area by these excellent financial ministries. Many of these believers are interested in this ministry because of their grace gifting. They may have the grace gifts of word of wisdom (1 Cor. 12:8) and/or exhortation (Rom. 12:8), combined with some experience in business where they had to create and manage budgets or do accounting work. While they may have been drawn to professions that give expression to their grace gifts, they are also motivated by the Spirit to minister to other believers in the areas in which they are gifted and experienced. They are a timely gift of God's grace when many Christians are very unwise in their financial decisions.[5]

My best friend, Chris Davis, worked for UPS for 29 years. He started working for UPS at age 18 and retired as an upper level executive at age 47. Why retire so early? In order to give more time to serving Christ in a wide variety of ways. On his path to success in business, Chris discovered that he had the grace gifts of exhortation and word of wisdom. He decided to develop these gifts—both of which flow out of one's biblical knowledge—by auditing several seminary courses. That's where I met Chris as one of his professors. We began a friendship that has deepened over the last several years. I've had a ringside seat in observing his rich business background combined with the gifts of wisdom and exhortation. How needed these gifts are to build up the body of Christ in love.

If Chris were a member at Last Organic, he would use his gifts in these areas to give wisdom to the family with $40,000 in credit card debt. Having taken advantage of the materials and training of various financial ministries, Chris would put quality resources into the hands of these financially challenged saints. Much like the debt counselor that the couple encountered in Chapter One, Chris helps people craft a specific plan to dig out of their financial hole. Unlike the debt counselor, however, Chris also educates these saints about the biblical perspective of money and possessions. It would be unthinkable from a biblical perspective to craft a five-year get-out-of-debt plan and exclude giving to the Lord as a part of the budget. Instead, Chris would suggest that the debt-reduction plan include giving to the Lord and saving a percentage of earnings. While such a plan could extend the amount of time needed to pay off the $40,000 in credit card debt, it would more importantly establish God-designed financial priorities.[6]

How many saints like Chris are we overlooking in our churches because of our impoverished view of gifting and our failure to equip not only the shepherds but the sheep? Our tradition of expecting our pastoral staff to have expertise in this area, among many, is not realistic. This is why we must nurture and equip the saints for the diverse requirements of ministry.

5. A young wife whose husband is on active duty with the military in the Middle East confesses that she has developed an emotional relationship with a co-worker.

So many times the life experience of the saints meshes so beautifully with their grace gifting. This has been my experience with believers who have experienced restoration from sexual sin. They know the pull toward sexual sin from the inside. They also know the devastation and deep sense of betrayal and guilt that comes with breaking the marriage covenant through adultery. The ministry of these battle-scarred veterans who have lived through such bitter sin and have then tasted the sweet fruit of repentance is a powerful one indeed—especially when it combines with their grace gifts. I have had the privilege of being in a local body with several such believers who have the gifts of exhortation (Rom. 12:8) and/or word of wisdom (1 Cor. 12:8). These saints bless the body of Christ with powerful counsel for those struggling with sexual sin.

When the lonely military wife steps up and admits her sin, she is also stepping into the restorative relational context of Last Organic. In particular, there is one mature, equipped saint who had helped shape the church's restorative values and who God had been preparing for many years to speak into this woman's life with great grace and candor. This older saint meets several times each week for a month, walking with the vulnerable wife as she breaks off the relationship with her co-worker. It is a very challenging time that demands a lot of intense, personal connecting, but it is fruitful. These intense counseling times are always undergirded with prayer by a group of prayer warriors in the body with the gift of faith (1 Cor. 12:9; 13:2). The counseling sister keeps them informed with daily updates so they can pray very specifically. These prayer warriors do not take lightly the Bible's coupling of exhortation and sin's deceitfulness: "But exhort one another every day, as long as it is called today, that none of you may be hardened by the deceitfulness of sin" (Heb. 3:13 ESV). They know this deceitfulness to be especially powerful with sexual sin, so they co-labor in the ministry to this lonely wife by expressing their gift of faith through targeted prayer. These differently gifted saints organically co-labor to build up the body of Christ in love by preserving this woman's marriage.

CONCLUSION

Sadly, it would be very difficult for a pastor or church staff member to justify the large investment of time that this mature woman and the prayer warriors gave this young wife. It would also have been difficult to justify the large amounts of time devoted to the Goth teenager, or the doubting college student, or the family with $40,000 in credit card debt. But why should crucial personal ministry be limited by the constraints of vocational Christian workers' job descriptions and corresponding time constraints? Why be limited by the grace gift mix of the vocational staff, which will almost certainly not be adequate for many situations? Why, indeed, when we have the overflowing resources of the rest of the Spirit-gifted saints in the sustainable organic body.

Only when we see *all* of the saints as part of "the ministry" can the full spectrum of the body's needs be adequately addressed. When the saints are nurtured and equipped to use their gifts in organic community with one another, the body builds itself up in love (Eph. 4:16). This is why the whole of the body's organic ministry is far greater than the sum of her parts. This is why the non-organic church pales in comparison to the organic church. If only we had eyes to see God's people with such gifting and the corresponding intention to nurture and equip them to walk accordingly: "For we are his workmanship, created in Christ Jesus for good works, which God prepared beforehand, that we should walk in them" (Eph. 2:10 ESV).

Chapter Four

A CHURCH WITHOUT LAITY

....

"The church is not like a bus, where passengers sit quietly and let someone else do the driving, but like an anthill, where everybody is at work."

–J. I. Packer[1]

Names are really significant in the Bible. Often they reveal the sense of a person's character and, in many cases, a person's mission or destiny. For example, when Israel asked for and got a king like other nations had, they got *Saul*, whose name means "asked for." By contrast, *David* means "beloved one" and he was sought out *by the Lord* to be Israel's second king because he was a man after God's own heart (1 Sam. 13:14). *Jesus* means "the Lord saves" because "it is He who will save His people from their sins" (Matt. 1:21). *Peter*, Jesus' key disciple, means "a stone or rock" (Greek, *Petros*). This meaning was the basis of Jesus' wordplay about the "large rock" (Greek, *petra*) upon which He would build His church when Peter confessed Jesus' messianic identity (Matt. 16:18).

Names are significant in our family also. We named our first child *Elizabeth* because it means "consecrated to God" and that was our prayer for her since before her birth. She has fulfilled her name's meaning in so many lovely ways. We gave our second child the name *Christopher* and prayed that he would have many years to live out the meaning of his name, "Christ-bearer." Unfortunately, it was at eighteen months of age that he bore the name of Christ through several amazing results from his untimely death. Our third child was an absolute "gift from the Lord," which is why we named him *Jonathan*. He has been a gift from God to us and many others throughout his life.

My wife of 42 years is named *Martha*, which means "lady or mistress of the house," just like *Martha* in Luke 10:38-42. My *Martha*, like her biblical model, is an amazingly competent woman in so many areas, an astonishing hostess, and the lovely person who has skillfully overseen our home since day one. However, when she was thirteen, a friend started calling her *Marty* and she liked that nickname much more than her given name of *Martha*. Fast-forward almost 50 years to the present. If you had the privilege of being with my wife for a short time, you would notice that she has grown into the name *Marty*. As she has matured in Christ, she has become equal parts of *Martha* + *Mary*. She has become *Mart-y*.

Regrettably, I don't have a biblical name. My first name is *Walter* and it is an Old German or Teutonic name that means "powerful warrior or army ruler." My middle name is *Bo* (from the Old French, *Beau*) and it means "handsome one." It is hard to write this without laughing, but I guess you could say, "I'm the whole package: a handsome mighty warrior." Now my wife is laughing, too.

There is a name that most Christians have been given that is not descriptive of their character or their mission: *laity* or *lay person*. It comes from the Greek word *laos* which simply means "people." Moreover, in a handful of its New Testament usages, *laos* casually contrasts *the people* from their leaders (e.g., Matt. 26:5), or from the Pharisees and scribes (e.g., Luke 7:29-30), or from the priests (e.g., Heb. 5:3). It is this last contrast—from the priests or clergy—that became the meaning of *laity* or *lay person* in the church. It has become a widely used term for Christians who are not ordained as pastors, priests or other vocational Christian workers.[2]

Laity is a horrifying misnomer for the vast majority of God's people. My goal in this chapter is to wrench it from your tightly clenched hands. While you may have described yourself as a *lay person* your whole life, it is not a name that accurately describes your character or mission in Christ.

By contrast, the most common name for followers of Jesus Christ in the Gospels and Acts is *disciples* (Greek, *mathētēs*; 267 times). In the epistles and in Revelation, the most common name is *saints* or "holy ones" (Greek, *hagioi*; 62 times).[3] To call the vast majority of Jesus' followers *laity* is to use a term that the New Testament does *not* use. But the greater problem is that we use a name that introduces an unbiblical hierarchy into God's people. By calling most saints *laity*, the term freezes and perpetuates an unbiblical contrast between the few who are "priestly" (like in Israel) and the vast majority who are not. Moreover, in this context the term *laity* is a contrasting term that emotionally connotes being "less than the special group." We introduce a myriad of theological problems into the body of Christ with such foul language.

I hope your first theological objection to the idea of laity is something like this: "But the New Testament teaches 'the priesthood of all believers,' so shouldn't we use language appropriate to viewing all of us in a 'priestly' role?" Well said. May I add to your good theologizing?

Jesus also specifically taught that we are not to use hierarchical language when referring to our leaders, "for One is your Teacher, *and you are all brothers [and sisters]*" (Matt. 23:8; my emphasis). Note that using such titles or names among Messiah

Jesus' people has two negative effects: it usurps God's role and it demeans our equality in Christ. In like manner, using the terms *laity* or *lay person* undercuts our equality in Christ by assigning diminished status to most Christians by implying elevated status for a few—the clergy.

I am not exaggerating when I say that I have not used the term *laity* in over 35 years, except to exhort God's people *not* to use it. When I use it in such a talk, every time I do, I turn and pretend to spit to clean out my mouth. As far as I am concerned, it is the foulest, unkindest, and most demeaning name that we could give to the Spirit-gifted saints of Christ's church. We are not *laity*, so please flush that word out of your Christian vocabulary!

The rest of this chapter and the next lay out the wonderfully positive view that God has of the *whole* body of Christ. He views all believers as organically sharing in the church's ministry. This ministry of all the saints is majestically described in a passage in Paul's Letter to the Ephesians. I'd like to guide you through Ephesians 4:11-16 and unpack its meaning and significance for our ministry as saints. First, let me establish a bit of context for this paragraph that begins the second half of Ephesians.

THE BROADER CONTEXT OF EPHESIANS

Ephesians 1-3 is a panoramic description of the new body (Eph. 2:13-16) that God has crafted through Jesus Christ. In these three chapters, Paul describes *our calling as saints* with these 36 breathtaking statements that are worthy of much contemplation:

We Are...

- chosen in Christ before the foundation of the world (1:4)

- made holy and blameless before God (1:4)

- predestined to adoption as sons [and daughters] of God (1:5)
- redeemed through Christ's blood (1:7)
- forgiven of our trespasses (1:7)
- made knowledgeable of the mystery of God's will (1:9)
- given an inheritance (1:11)
- sealed in Christ with the Holy Spirit (1:13)
- given the Holy Spirit as a pledge of our inheritance (1:14)
- given riches of glory as an inheritance (1:18)
- possessing surpassing greatness in His power toward us (1:19)
- put under the Headship of the all-powerful Christ in the church (1:20-23)
- made recipients of God's rich mercy and great love (2:4)
- made alive from our deadness in sin (2:5)
- enlivened, raised up, and seated with Christ in the heavenly places (2:5-6)
- made future trophies of His rich grace (2:7)
- saved by grace through faith not works (2:8-9)
- made God's workmanship--created for good works (2:10)
- brought near to God by the blood of Christ (2:13)
- freed from the dividing wall that separated us from God and His people (2:14)
- freed from the enmity of the Law abolished in Christ's death (2:15)

- reconciled with believing Jews and Gentiles into a new body (2:16)
- given access to God in the Holy Spirit (2:18)
- made a fellow citizen and household member of God's family (2:19)
- built upon the foundation of the apostles and prophets (2:20)
- being fitted and growing into a holy temple in the Lord (2:21)
- being built into a dwelling of God in the Spirit (2:22)
- made fellow heirs and fellow body members with the saints (3:6)
- made fellow partakers of the promise in Christ (3:6)
- made proclaimers of the manifold wisdom of God to angelic beings (3:10)
- given boldness and confident access to God through faith in Christ (3:12)
- given access to the Holy Spirit's power in our inner person (3:16)
- given the capacity for our hearts to be Christ's dwelling place (3:17)
- given the potential to comprehend Christ's unlimited love for us (3:18-19)
- given the potential to be filled up to the fullness of God (3:20)
- made partakers of His exceedingly abundant powers (3:21)

How could we possibly live up to such a lofty calling? That is exactly the answer that Ephesians 4-6 gives, beginning with Paul's exhortation in Ephesians 4:1: "Therefore I, the prisoner of the Lord, implore you to walk in a manner worthy of the calling with which you have been called." The lofty calling of the saints in Ephesians 1-3 demands a lofty walking/living by those same saints in Ephesians 4-6. Ephesians 4:1-16 introduces the first of several facets of this magnificent walk.

THE CONTENT OF EPHESIANS 4:1-16

This robust paragraph begins the description of our worthy walk as saints by emphasizing that we *walk in unity*. Because of its length and complexity, I've broken the biblical unit of thought into the three sub-units that develop its unity theme:

4:1-6 – *All believers* are to walk in unity/oneness that reflects the Trinity's oneness.

> [1]Therefore I, the prisoner of the Lord, implore you to walk in a manner worthy of the calling with which you have been called, [2]with all humility and gentleness, with patience, showing tolerance for one another in love, [3]being diligent to preserve the unity of the Spirit in the bond of peace. [4]*There is* one body and one Spirit, just as also you were called in one hope of your calling; [5]one Lord, one faith, one baptism, [6]one God and Father of all who is over all and through all and in all.

4:7-10 – Our unity is manifested in the diversity of Christ's grace gifts *to each of us.*

> [7]But to each one of us grace was given according to the measure of Christ's gift. [8]Therefore it says,
>
> > "WHEN HE ASCENDED ON HIGH,
> >
> > HE LED CAPTIVE A HOST OF CAPTIVES,

AND HE GAVE GIFTS TO MEN."

[9](Now this *expression,* "He ascended," what does it mean except that He also had descended into the lower parts of the earth? [10]He who descended is Himself also He who ascended far above all the heavens, so that He might fill all things.)

4:11-16 – Unity for *all of us* out of the grace-gifted diversity of *each of us* is possible because of the ministry of *some of us* who equip the saints for their ministry.

[11]And He gave some *as* apostles, and some *as* prophets, and some *as* evangelists, and some *as* pastors and teachers, [12]for the equipping of the saints for the work of service, to the building up of the body of Christ; [13]until we all attain to the unity of the faith, and of the knowledge of the Son of God, to a mature man, to the measure of the stature which belongs to the fullness of Christ. [14]As a result, we are no longer to be children, tossed here and there by waves and carried about by every wind of doctrine, by the trickery of men, by craftiness in deceitful scheming; [15]but speaking the truth in love, we are to grow up in all *aspects* into Him who is the head, *even* Christ, [16]from whom the whole body, being fitted and held together by what every joint supplies, according to the proper working of each individual part, causes the growth of the body for the building up of itself in love.

If given the choice, I doubt that most of us would place *unity* as the first, and perhaps most important descriptor of the saints' lifestyle. We are far more concerned about our individual rights than the unity of the body of Christ. We assert and protect our personal rights first and then, if we have any time and energy left, we weakly add that we should be unified. This is unfortunate, because the New Testament expresses exactly the opposite value-structure. It places unity at the top and individual rights way down the line (e.g., 1 Cor. 8-10 and Rom. 14:1-15:13). This adds weight to the significance of beginning the description of the saints' worthy walk by underscoring that it is a walk in the unity of the body. Moreover, note the shift in focus from *all of us* to *each of us* to *some of us* and then back again to *all of us* as Paul develops the unity theme within this complex paragraph:

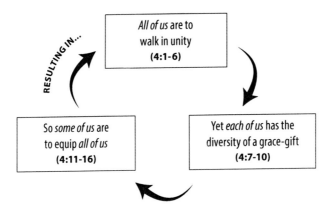

CONCLUSION

There is much we could learn about preserving the Spirit-crafted unity of the body of Christ by studying Ephesians 4:1-6. Additionally, unpacking 4:7-10 and the nature of Christ's victorious gifting of His people with grace-gifts would be most edifying.[4] However, in light of this book's specific topic, our focus will be on the special role of releasing and equipping the saints that *some* grace-gifted persons are to have in the body of Christ in 4:11-16. But before we begin that focus, it is important to remember the threefold thrust of this chapter:

- The most common New Testament terms for Christians are *disciples* (of Jesus) and *saints* ("holy ones"); the term *laity* is unbiblical and a horrific misnomer that demeans the dignity and designed ministry of Jesus' Spirit-gifted followers.

- The dignity deeded to those who believe in Jesus in Ephesians 1-3 is astonishing in its breadth and depth and is *a weighty calling* that demands *an equally weighty walk* in Ephesians 4-6.

- The first and perhaps preeminent characteristic of our worthy walk in Christ is that we walk in a manner that mirrors the amazing *unity* expressed by the Trinity (Eph. 4:1-6) as well as the dizzying *diversity* of Jesus' grace-gifts to each of us (Eph. 4:7-10).

Our only hope for making this all come together is that *some* of the grace-gifted saints fulfill their Jesus-assigned role *to release and equip the saints* (Eph. 4:11-12). Fulfilling this task will replace the non-organic, unsustainable church. It is to that biblical task that we now turn.

Chapter Five

A CHURCH WHERE ALL MINISTER

....

Note the use of the term "minister" in a recent ad in a national Christian magazine:

If you are…

- A minister in charge of a church
- A leader having recognized pastoral care over a group of people
- A retired minister
- A credentialed minister currently without a congregation
- A Bible college student or minister-in-training

According to this ad, which reflects the widespread understanding of what and who a "minister" is in the non-organic church, we learn several things about those who minister:

- they are "in charge of a church,"
- they have "recognized pastoral care over a group of people,"
- they can be "retired,"
- they are "credentialed" and can be "without a congregation,"
- and by going to a certain type of school, they can be a "minister-in-training."

The long-held view that a "minister" is someone who is paid to do "the ministry" and who is in charge of everyone else in the church is absolutely and totally *without any foundation* in the New Testament. This is a fabrication of early church history that continues the priestly tradition of the Old Testament with the added bonus of a paycheck. We then feel no qualms about reading this fabrication back into the New Testament. We turn the perfectly good Greek word *diakoneō*, meaning "to serve or minister to," into a paid profession.

For example, I just looked up every occurrence of the verb *diakoneō* ("to serve or minister to") in the New Testament, along with its corresponding noun *diakonia* ("service or ministry"). My results raised some interesting and funky questions:

- Were *the angels* who *ministered to* Jesus in the wilderness paid? (Matt. 4:11; Mark 1:13)?

- Was *Peter's mother-in-law* paid when Jesus healed her and she *served* food to them [as a waitress?] (Matt. 8:15; Mark 1:31; Luke 4:39)?

- Were *the grateful women* who were *ministering to* Jesus by paying for His disciples' and His food and shelter out of their own means paid [back?] (Luke 8:1-3, especially v. 3)?

- Did *the apostles* move into a higher pay bracket when they left *the ministering of food/tables* [as waiters?] (Acts 6:1-2) for *the ministering of the word* (Acts 6:4)?

I hope you see the absurdity of thinking that *those who serve or minister* should be viewed as professionals. It has nothing to do with a profession and everything to do with serving God by loving and caring for people. Do you agree that all Christians should serve and minister to others? If you do, then you must also admit *that all of us who know Christ are a part of His ministry to others* and this means that *all of us are ministers (servants) of Christ.* Treat it as a relatively insignificant fact that some are graciously freed up by God's people to use the gifts Jesus gave them to minister to others as their vocation. They're not in *full-time Christian service* and the rest of us are not in *part-time Christian service.* We're all serving Christ as our life's highest calling and some of us just happen to be paid to do so.

A WORD FOR ALL "MINISTERS/SERVANTS"

In the previous chapter, we saw that Ephesians 1-3 chronicles God's amazing work in Christ of crafting believing Jews and believing Gentiles into a new organism—the body of Christ (Eph. 2:14-16). It is a lofty calling that demands a lofty lifestyle. We are to walk in a manner worthy of our calling in Christ (4:1). Such a worthy walk begins when we *walk in unity.*

Ephesians 4:1-16 explains that our walking in unity…

- reflects the Trinity's oneness (4:1-6),

- comes out of our individual Christ-gifted diversity (4:7-10), and

- is only possible when *some* of those gifted individuals fulfill their God-given job description to equip the saints for the work of ministry (4:11-16).

This chapter unpacks the strategic focus and astonishing impact of *some* of the gifted saints on the rest of the body of Christ.

THE ROLE OF "SOME" IN EQUIPPING THE SAINTS
(EPHESIANS 4:11-12)

It is a daunting task for all the saints to walk in unity in the midst of the astonishing diversity of our grace-gifts. When we include our ethnic and cultural differences, our personalities, our personal histories and our educational differences, the task can become overwhelming. This is why the special ministry of *some* in the midst of all of us is so vital. These gifted members of the body of Christ have a very special job description in undergirding the organic walk in unity. Listen again Paul's words in Ephesians 4:11-12: "And He gave some *as* apostles, and some *as* prophets, and some *as* evangelists, and some *as* pastors and teachers, for the equipping of the saints for the work of service, to the building up of the body of Christ."

Note that Paul's point in these verses is that "a specific expression of Christ's grace to us is the fourfold cluster of gifted individuals who are to equip all other believers to use their respective grace gifts to build up the Church." If this is true, then you can begin to see why it is so very inappropriate to use the term *laity* to describe most of God's grace-gifted people. But I'm jumping ahead of myself. Let me explain what Paul is saying here.

In Ephesians 4:11 Paul boldly states that Christ's victorious gifting of His church in verses 7-10 includes these *four* groups of individuals with the *specific spiritual gifting* as apostles, prophets, evangelists and pastor-teachers.[1] Some speak of the so-called "fivefold gifting" in this verse because they separate the gifts of *pastor* and *teacher* from one another. However, looking at verse 11 in English, we note that Paul's listing of these groups changes when he gets to the last two gifts of *pastors* and *teachers*. His grammar seems to be pointing toward viewing them as connected to one another since they stand under the same article ("the") in Greek. The ESV translation of verse 11 captures this subtlety: "And he gave the apostles, the prophets, the evangelists, *the pastors and teachers*" (my emphasis). There are good grammatical reasons for viewing the last gifted group as having *a dual-focus*: pastoring (shepherding) and teaching (i.e., *pastor-teachers* or *shepherd-teachers*.)[2] The so-called "fivefold gifting" is actually fourfold.

However, there is a much more debated theological point in verse 11 that we need to mention. This is the issue of whether Jesus is still giving apostles and prophets to His church. There are many wonderful evangelicals who argue that passages like Ephesians 2:19-22 state that *apostles* and *prophets* were a part of the foundation of the church (2:20) and therefore *ceased* to exist with the death of the original apostles early in the second century. There is another version of this view called *cessationism*, which generally argues that seven other grace-gifts, in addition to the two mentioned in Ephesians, also ceased. These nine gifts are viewed by cessationists as either *foundational* (apostles, prophets, word of knowledge, and word of wisdom) or *confirmatory* of the apostles and their gospel message (miracles, healing, tongues, interpreting of tongues and discerning of spirits). I've already mentioned this issue briefly in an endnote in *Chapter Three* and I address it a bit more in depth in *Appendix #1*. I have been on both sides of the theological fence regarding this discussion, so I can understand and empathize with the conflicting views.[3]

We don't need to settle this issue to understand Ephesians 4:11-16. We still benefit from the gifting of apostles and prophets whether they laid the foundation of the church in the first century or whether they continue in the church to the present. Their gifting fulfills the task of equipping the saints in either interpretation.

The more important issue for us is the job description given by Jesus to these four groups of individuals in Ephesians 4:12. It is immensely important to see the flow of thought and understand the grammatical and logical connections of the key prepositional phrases in this verse. Unfortunately, the theological assumptions of the clergy/laity distinction have blurred Paul's logical progression for many commentators. What follows is the most straightforward and defensible understanding of Paul's grammar in this crucial verse. My expanded translation especially emphasizes the sense of the Greek prepositional connectives:

(4:11)   And *He* [*Jesus* from vv. 7-8; emphatic]

gave [cf. v. 8]

some to be apostles,

and some to be prophets,

and some to be evangelists,

and some to be pastor-teachers,

(4:12)   *for the immediate purpose* of the equipping of the saints

for the goal of doing the work of ministry/service

to the ultimate goal of the building up of the body of Christ.

Paul's grammar could not be any more pointed as to what is *the conscious, overt, specific purpose* of these gifted members of the body. When they exercise their respective grace-gifts, apostles, prophets, evangelists and pastor-teachers should have the collective thrust of equipping all believers so that they can do the work of ministering/serving in Christ's name and thereby build up the body of Christ.[4]

According to Ephesians 4:12, one of the key things that the Lord will ask these four gifted groups when they stand before Him is *not* "How well did you minister *with your gifts?*" Rather, He will ask, "How well did *the saints minister with their gifts* after you equipped them to do so?" Given this scenario, it is immensely important to understand what *equipping* means. The

Greek word behind our translation *equipping* is *katartismos*. In extra-biblical Greek, it is somewhat of a medical technical term for "the setting of a bone" or "the restoration of a shoulder." Closely related is the Greek word *katartizō*, its verbal form in the New Testament, which means "to put in order or restore." It is used of the disciples putting their fishing nets back into their proper condition before fishing again (Matt. 4:21; Mark 1:19) and of Christians "restoring or putting back in order" a sinning brother or sister (Gal. 6:1). In addition to Galatians 6:1, a case could be made that Paul's other four usages of the verbal form of this word mean "be joined together or be put in order" (Rom. 9:22; 1 Cor. 1:10; 2 Cor. 13:11; and 1 Thess. 3:10).

All of this demonstrates that the core idea of *equipping* is "to put in order or proper condition; to make complete or adequate by joining together." This means that *equipping the saints* is a bit more specific that just training them, although it includes that dimension. More precisely, *equipping the saints* in Ephesians 4:11-16 means helping them be set in proper order within the body of Christ. To equip the saints is to help them discover their grace-gifts from Jesus (Eph. 4:7-10) and to begin to use them by being joined together in organic community with other saints. It is helping believers discover what members or parts of the body they are and then helping them begin to fulfill those functions in Christ's church. In a very real sense, the four gifted groups in Ephesians 4:11 act as the four corner pieces of a large jigsaw puzzle. They know their specific place and provide the perspective to fit the other pieces into their places in the puzzle.

To equip the saints is to help them discover and grow in their competency *to minister* by using their grace gifts. Note the language that Paul uses for expressing *the purpose* of the arranging of the saints in 4:12: "for the work of *ministry* or *service* (Greek, *diakonia*)." I cannot resist underscoring the tragic irony of the terminology in this phrase. While our ecclesiastical traditions demean the vast majority of God's people with the name of *laity*, God bestows a far different name on them: *ministers*. It is *the saints* who are *the ministers* because they are the ones designed to do *the work of ministry*. I don't think that God ever intended for us to make *ministry/ministers* into technical vocational terms like we have done. The New Testament teaches that the ministry of the church is *an every-member-ministry*. This is the biblical outworking of the priesthood of all believers. When the saints are nurtured and equipped—when they find and fulfill their organic role in Christ's body—then *they* build up the body both quantitatively and qualitatively, as Ephesians 4:12 states. This is why being a church without laity is so immensely important. We need a fully equipped body to achieve maximum quantitative and qualitative growth. This is what transforms the non-organic church into the sustainable church.

A SHOCKING LETTER

A few years ago I joined a large evangelical church and received the typical new member's letter from the senior pastor. I was only in the second paragraph when I began to react negatively to its content. It read something like this: "It is important to me and my ministry that you attend each Sunday morning service." The next paragraph deepened my angst when I read, "Your attendance at the Sunday evening services is also very important to me and my ministry." The next paragraph put me over the top when I read, "Being at the Wednesday evening services is also a vital way to support me in my ministry." I would like to say that I pulled this letter from my files and quoted from it in writing this paragraph. However, I couldn't do that because I ripped it up the moment I read it!

Somewhere this pastor got the idea that all of us fellow saints were there *to support him in his ministry.* My problem was that I knew too much of the New Testament's teaching: that the apostles, prophets, evangelists and pastor-teachers were Jesus' gifts to His people t*o support them in their ministries.* I guess it was the 1,900 years of church traditions that had emboldened this brother to invert the biblical perspective. He very confidently asserted that my presence in the church was largely *for his benefit.* His large non-organic church was filled with dear saints who had been persuaded that they were simply *lay people* whose grand role in the scheme of things was to support *their minister as he did the ministry.* He ministered while they quietly prayed and paid. How tragic and demeaning to God's people. These saints had no idea that each one of them had been given grace-gifts through Jesus' spiritual conquest and that they should be using them to do the work of ministry. Likely, such thoughts would have been viewed as radically subversive and only intended to disrupt the passive state of the vast majority of those in the non-organic church which bears the name *laity.*

THE GOAL AND RESULTS OF NURTURED, EQUIPPED SAINTS (EPHESIANS 4:13-16)

Our ministry as saints who have been equipped is to result in the ultimate goal of a unified and mature church according to Ephesians 4:13: "until we all attain to the unity of the faith, and of the knowledge of the Son of God, to a mature man, to the measure of the stature which belongs to the fullness of Christ."

Note that verse 13 states that our goal is *a group goal* that is stated in terms of what we all should do. Paul's language is the language of being on a journey, all of us moving toward and arriving at the same destination: the unity of the faith, the knowledge of the Son of God and the full maturity of the whole body of Christ (viewed as a single person). There is no room for Lone Ranger Christianity. I love this sailing analogy: "We are all lashed to the same mast!" We will sail or sink together. This is why divisions, jealousy and strife are such deadly viruses among God's people (e.g., 1 Cor. 3:1-4). Our goal is a unified maturity.

If we are traveling toward this destination, what will the church look like? We should be displaying *the marks of spiritual maturity*. Paul completes this amazing paragraph by expressing three of these marks in Ephesians 4:14-16. I have inserted the description of each mark within the biblical text of this passage:

Mark #1: We should have a *doctrinal or theological stability.*

[14]As a result, we are no longer to be children, tossed here and there by waves and carried about by every wind of doctrine, by the trickery of men, by craftiness in deceitful scheming;

Mark #2: We should have *mature, loving communication of the truth.*

[15]but speaking the truth in love, we are to grow up in all *aspects* into Him who is the head, *even* Christ,

Mark #3: We should have *the healthy, loving functioning of every Christian in the body (church).*

[16]from whom the whole body, being fitted and held together by what every joint supplies, according to the proper working of each individual part, causes the growth of the body for the building up of itself in love.

Ephesians 4:14 pictures immature Christians ("children") who are made spiritual "leaves in the wind" by two storm pictures: the pounding theological surf and the shifting winds of false teachings. Behind this corrupt theology is the "trickery" or "cunning" of persons whose ends justify any means ("craftiness") and who are adept at various deceptive strategies ("deceitful scheming"). This is why cultists love to knock on Christians' doors—because most of the saints are doctrinally ungrounded due to their defective knowledge of the Bible and theology. God's *unequipped* saints become windswept leaves, picked up and carried about by the current expressions of faulty theology: it's all about me, prosperity theology, New Age spiritualism, etc. One result of the equipping process is that this immaturity is replaced by a steadfast biblical and theological knowledge in the midst of spiritual storms. This is the first mark of spiritual maturity among saints who are being equipped.

The second mark is the presence of *mature, loving communication of the truth* in v. 15: "but speaking the truth in love, we are to grow up in all *aspects* into Him who is the head, *even* Christ." In contrast to the picture of getting tossed around as spiritual children in v. 14, equipped saints are capable of entering the marketplace and communicating the truth of God and His Word to their listeners in a loving manner. Paul expresses this communication by making a verb out of the noun "truth." He literally says that we should be *truthing in/with love*. Given that Paul normally uses the term *truth* when he is speaking of the gospel message, it is very likely that he is focusing on the church's external communication of the gospel—truth—rather than just our internal communication with one another. He will address the internal communication in Ephesians 4:25. In v. 15 we see the contrast between being overwhelmed in the world's tumultuous spiritual context (v. 14) versus the balanced expression of the gospel with both love and truth within that same spiritually chaotic setting (v. 15). Just like a baby's body grows to catch up with his or her proportionally large head, so does the sustainable church grow up in our proclaiming of the gospel to match our head Jesus Christ. He is grace, truth and love personified.

In Ephesians 4:16 Paul sets forth a third mark of spiritual maturity: *the healthy, loving functioning of every member of the body*. Notice Paul's threefold emphasis on this expression of whole-body involvement:

> "from whom *the whole body*, being fitted and held together by what *every joint supplies*, according to the proper working of *each individual part*, causes the growth of the body for the building up of itself in love" (my emphasis).

As each believer is under the control of the head of the body, he or she will experience the joy of being harmoniously "fitted together," as Paul uses the language of a stonemason putting a stone in place (cf. Eph. 2:21). Additionally, every body "ligament" (a better translation than "joint") is to help to "knit or hold together" fellow body members, as Paul uses a biological analogy. In other words we see a synergistic organic working of the body of Christ: Jesus, the head, is working in and through each body part that is functioning in obedience by contributing to the building up of the body when she or he uses her or his grace-gift in a loving manner.

Imagine the difference in synergistic effect between 90-100% of the body members fulfilling their bodily functions versus 10-20%. Jesus has assigned organic body functions to every believer in Him (4:7). However, the vast majority of these saints apparently never discover and fulfill their roles. Why? Because *some* of the gifted saints (Eph. 4:11) fail to equip the rest of the saints "for the work of service, to the building up of the body of Christ" (Eph. 4:12).

CONCLUSION: WHAT WE LOSE BY *NOT* EQUIPPING THE SAINTS

It is tragically easy to enumerate the losses that the body of Christ suffers if we do not nurture and equip the saints to do the work of ministry. However, I'm going to limit myself to listing the losses we accrue by not experiencing the fruitfulness that is mentioned in Ephesians 4:11-16. By neglecting to equip the saints to discover and use their grace-gifts, these are our losses:

- 4:12 – The saints cannot do the work of *their ministry* of building up the body of Christ.

- 4:13a – We frustrate the goal of a unified church.

- 4:13b – We frustrate the goal of the full knowledge of Christ

- 4:14-16 – We deprive the body of:

  o theological stability (4:14)

  o loving evangelism (4:15)

  o every-member-ministry (4:16)

These are *devastating* losses. What astonishes me is that God gives us the freedom to go our own stubborn and traditional way of doing church or to chase every fad and new pragmatic technique for drawing a big crowd—think the non-organic church. The common factor of our traditionalism and our faddism is that we continue to ignore what His Word says about how we should function. We have explored the lunatic fringe of this freedom. The non-organic church is unsustainable. This is why we need to be a church without *laity*. We should recognize that we are a much-blessed people by God in Christ. A grand part of Messiah's conquest over Satan and his demonic host is that Jesus poured out His victor's bounty upon His people by giving us grace-gifts (Eph. 4:7-10). We should now be about the work of discovering, using and growing in these marvelous gifts. *This is the work of equipping the saints.* It is the work of helping every believer find his or her role within the body of Christ so that we can be about the work of ministry together (Eph. 4:12). To do any less is to continue to deny the dignity of the people of God, a people well worth equipping.

Remember and take to heart...

> "The church is not like a bus, where passengers sit quietly and let someone else do the driving, but like an anthill, where everybody is at work."

> **–J. I. Packer**[5]

Chapter Six

GROWING MINISTRY AROUND THE SHEEP, NOT JUST THE SHEPHERDS

....

This is part of a recent email I received from the pastor of men's ministry at an evangelical church after I spoke about "Equipping the Saints": *"I was completely blown away by what you shared with us. I've been in the church my whole, entire life and, regrettably, we just don't hear this stuff!"*

Perhaps your response to the first five chapters is similar to this dear brother's. You may be saying to yourself, "Walt, your view of the church sounds too good to be true. If it is true, then why haven't I heard 'this stuff' before?" There's a very good reason you haven't heard it: *Tradition.* We have over 1,900 years of Christian traditions that have emphasized that the focal point of the ministry of the church is *the leaders—the [supposed] ministers.* This is the core theological belief of the non-organic church.

Remember the five-fold description of "a minister" in a recent ad in a national Christian magazine that was noted in Chapter Five? Its first assumption is that "a minister is in charge of a church."

I have been teaching at theological schools/seminaries for the last 28 years. I confess that I lie awake at night agonizing over the meta-message that we continue to communicate to the church's future leaders. We collectively tell them in innumerable ways, "You are training to be *a minister* and you grow the local church's ministry around *your* gifts." There is only a very small emphasis on equipping the saints at large to use their gifts. Seminary graduates all over the world walk away from their respective schools with this traditional understanding which frames the life of the church primarily as an *institution*, rather than as an *organism*. The following diagram shows in vivid contrasting fashion how the conceptual framework of the non-organic church misses the organic, every-member ministry:

THE CHURCH

AS AN INSTITUTION	AS AN ORGANISM
1. **Starting Point:** The leadership offices in the church. The true church is found where:	1. **Starting Point:** The Body of Christ. The church is the whole people of God in whom Christ dwells.
a. The Word of God is rightly proclaimed	2. **Bottom-up:** The church's ministry is shaped by the gifts and callings distributed by the Holy Spirit to the whole body of Christ.
b. The ordinances are rightly administered	
2. **Top-down:** The "ministry" is the province of the ordained offices of the church ("the clergy/ministers").	3. **All God's people are to minister!** The New Testament makes no *laity* distinction. All ministry is to be by all the saints.
3. **"Lay ministry":** It supplements and is secondary to ordained ministry.	4. **Our Unity:** *One* people (all of whom are gifted) with *one* ministry.[1]
4. **Our "Unity":** Two peoples (clergy versus laity) with *two* distinct ministries (ordained versus lay).	

Those who serve in parachurch organizations also follow the philosophy of building ministry around their own gifts. However, the parachurch ministries temper it a bit by adding, "You build your ministry around *our parachurch organization's primary emphases.*" Of course, the parachurch staff member would not be serving with a particular ministry unless his or her grace-gifts matched the organization's spiritual emphases. Nevertheless, in many ways this also thwarts the organic life and ministry of the saints. We'll look at this more in Chapter Ten.

The beginning of the non-organic church—the church's tradition to grow ministry primarily around the shepherds and not the sheep—is first chronicled in AD 56 when Paul wrote 1 Corinthians 1:10-17. He rebukes the Corinthians for being divisive by inappropriately championing various leaders: "I am of Paul," and "I am of Apollos," and "I am of Cephas," and "I [am] of Christ" (v. 12b). Paul addresses this leader-fixation by correcting the Corinthians' misunderstanding of *the spiritual nature of the gospel message* (1 Cor. 1:18-2:16) and their missed identification of *the servant-nature of the gospel messengers* (1 Cor. 3-4). I find it fascinating that the most thorough discussion of grace-gifts in the New Testament is also in this letter: 1 Corinthians 12-14. In addition to correcting the Corinthians' abuse of some gifts and overly glorifying others, Paul was also teaching them how to grow healthy, balanced organic ministry around *the gifts of all the sheep*, not just around those of the shepherds.

The post-New Testament movement toward a shepherd-centered ministry began within fifteen years of the writing of the last New Testament book (Revelation in AD 95/96). It started when a church leader named Ignatius of Antioch wrote seven extant letters as he was being led to Rome to be martyred for his Christian faith in AD 110. From this heroic church leader, we have the beginning of the post-apostolic shift away from the New Testament's model of organic, every-member ministry to the institutional model of building ministry around the leader. He advocated for the first time a "mono-episcopate" or single *bishop/overseer* (Greek, *episkopos*) to lead Christian communities instead of the plurality of *elders* (Greek, *presbuteroi*). Listen to Ignatius' epochal advice to the church in Smyrna:

> You must all follow the bishop, as Jesus Christ followed the Father... *Let no one do anything that has to do with the church without the bishop.* Only that Eucharist [the Lord's Supper] which is under the authority of the bishop (or whomever he himself designates) is to be considered valid. (2) Wherever the bishop appears, there let the congregation be, just as wherever Jesus Christ is, there is the catholic [universal] church. It is not permissible either to baptize or to hold a love feast without the bishop. But whatever he approves is also pleasing to God, in order that everything you do may be trustworthy and valid. (*To the Smyrnaeans* 8; my emphasis)[2]

Note that according to this view, there is no church without the overseer. There are no valid ordinances—Lord's Supper and baptism—without the ordained leader. There is no valid love feast that encompasses the Lord's Supper (see Jude 12) without the credentialed overseer. This theology advocates that you can have lots of sheep and not be the church. No ordained leadership, no church. This hierarchical leadership model developed rather quickly into the institutional conception of the church pictured above. It is shared by Roman Catholicism, Eastern Orthodoxy and Protestantism. From it has flowed the artificial and unbiblical distinction between the leaders—eventually called *clergy*—and the rest of God's people—eventually called *laity*. The seeds of institutionalization were sown very early in the post-apostolic life of the church and grew vigorously in the hierarchical cultures of the Mediterranean world. Our institutional conception of how we do church—the non-organic church—is an ancient tradition that has pervaded all expressions of Christianity for over 1,900 years. Its growth has essentially choked the organic life out of the church.

However, my primary goal is not to criticize our traditional model. Rather, in this chapter and the next two, I want to present the hopeful alternative—the New Testament data about the grace-gifts given for every-member ministry. In Chapter Seven we'll answer a few crucial questions about how these gifts enable us to build the church's organic ministry around all the sheep, rather than around a handful of vocational shepherds.

GRACE-GIFTS IN THE NEW TESTAMENT

The Key Lists: Romans 12:6-8; Ephesians 4:11; 1 Peter 4:10-11; 1 Corinthians 12:6-10/12:28/12:29-30/13:1-3/13:8/14:6/14:26

THE 19 GRACE-GIFTS BY PASSAGE

ROMANS 12:6-8	EPHESIANS 4:11	1 PETER 4:10-11
• Prophecy	• Apostles	• Speaking
• Service/ministry	• Prophets	• Serving/ministering
• Teaching	• Evangelists	
• Exhortation	• Pastor-teachers	
• Giving		
• Leading		
• Showing mercy		

1 CORINTHIANS 12:6-10	1 CORINTHIANS 12:28	1 CORINTHIANS 12:29-30
• Word of wisdom	• Apostles	• Apostles
• Word of knowledge	• Prophets	• Prophets
• Faith	• Teachers	• Teachers
• Gifts of healings	• Miracles	• *Workers of* miracles
• Miracles/works of power	• Gifts of healings	• Gifts of healings
• Prophecy	• Helps	• Speaking with tongues
• Distinguishing between spirits	• Administrations	• Interpreting of tongues
• Kinds of tongues	• Kinds of Tongues	
• Interpreting of tongues		

1 CORINTHIANS 13:1-3, 8 *(a more casual list)*	1 CORINTHIANS 14:6 *(a more casual list)*	1 CORINTHIANS 14:26 *(a more casual list)*
• Tongues (two times)	• Tongues	• Has a psalm
• Prophecy (two times)	• Revelation	• Teaching
• Know mysteries	• Knowledge	• Revelation
• Knowledge (two times)	• Prophecy	• Tongues
• Faith	• Teaching	• Interpreting of tongues
• Giving		

As you look at the lists that flow right out of the biblical text, you will note that some of the lists focus on the grace-gifts themselves (e.g., *prophecy* and *teaching* in Rom. 12:6-7), while other lists focus on the persons who exercise those gifts (e.g., *prophets* and *teachers* in 1 Cor. 12:28). Both the gifts and the persons are gracious endowments from Jesus to His church. Mindful of this, I will usually refer to them with the primary term the New Testament uses—*grace-gifts*—rather than the more popular term—*spiritual gifts*.

Perhaps as you look at the lists, a couple of questions come to mind. For example, "Do we have a complete list of grace-gifts?" This is easy to answer: "No" and "Yes". I say "No" because no two lists agree in language, number or character of the gifts. The lists also seem to be addressing specific local church situations and are probably representational, not exhaustive. For example, the list in 1 Peter 4:10-11 seems to be a summary of two different *categories* of gifts, rather than a list of the gifts themselves. Additionally, there is great flexibility in Paul's (and Peter's) use of language on these matters in the New Testament. When all is said and done, we must remember that these gifts represent *ministries* and ministries have an inherent fluidity.[3]

However, I must also say "Yes, *functionally* we probably do have a complete list because these lists of ministries do cover about everything in the life and work of the church." This is especially true when we see the combinations of multiple grace-gifts in the saints' lives. These gift combinations bring diversity and flexibility to the various ministries that the saints can have. In my experience, most believers have at least two grace-gifts and many times three. Mathematically speaking, this results in a very large variety of ministries given the number of potential gift combinations among the 19 gifts. Functionally, one would be hard-pressed to conceive of any ministry that could not be implemented out of a combination of two or three of the 19 gifts that we have listed in the New Testament.

A second question that arises when we look at the gift lists is this: "Do other passages mention additional gifts in passing?" Specifically, *celibacy* is called a *gift* (Greek, *charisma*) in 1 Corinthians 7:7 and *being hospitable* is mentioned in 1 Peter 4:9, just before Peter's gift list in 4:10-11.

The context of 1 Peter 4:7-9 is a triad of exhortations to cultivate *specific virtues* in the Christian life since "the end of all things is near" (v. 7a). These are virtues that all Christians should cultivate: 1) be of sound judgment and sober spirit for prayer (v. 7b), 2) be fervent in love for one another (v. 8), and 3) *"Be hospitable* to one another without complaint" in v. 9 (my emphasis). Contextually, *hospitality* is not a grace-gift listed with other grace-gifts. While I'm not ready to go the wall with my conclusion, this lack of being in one of the gift lists moves me away from thinking that there is a specific gift of *hospitality*. Instead, it seems to be *a virtue* that *all Christians* should develop. Amazing things have happened in history when we do.[4]

Seeing *celibacy* as a grace-gift in 1 Corinthians 7:7 is a common interpretive mistake. The mistake is *assuming* that a word is a technical term *in this passage* because it may have had a more technical meaning *in other passages*. The discussion is about marriage, not spiritual gifts in 1 Corinthians 7. The Apostle Paul culminates his discussion of singleness and marriage in 7:1-7 by saying this in verse 7: "Yet I wish that all men were even as I myself am. However, each man has his own *gift* from God, one in this manner and another in that." In this marriage context, Paul uses the word *gift* very casually—not technically—to refer to the fact that God gives to some the special capacity to live a life of celibacy/singleness like he was doing and to others the gift of a mate. If *celibacy* is a grace-gift in this context, then getting married and having a mate is also a grace-gift. Obviously, Paul is not using *gift* with this sort of technical meaning in 1 Corinthians 7:7 as he does elsewhere. Noting *the context* of 7:7 makes this clear. Ignoring the context and *assuming* a more technical meaning for *gift* confuses it.

It is obvious that I am arguing more cautiously by basing my final number of grace-gifts only on those that are mentioned in the gift lists. While others argue for as many as 27 gifts, the New Testament passages only include 19 spiritual gifts in the six more formal lists and in the four very casual lists in 1 Corinthians 13:3, 8 and 14:6, 26. However, to give you some idea of how others count the total of gifts, see the final gift tally of these five popular spiritual gifts' books:

- **27 gifts** – C. Peter Wagner, *Finding Your Spiritual Gifts, Updated and Expanded* (Regal Books, 1979, 1985, 1995, 2005). Wagner uses the popular "Wagner-Modified Houts Questionnaire" that includes eight more gifts like *missionary* and *hospitality* (p. 10) and *voluntary poverty, celibacy, intercession, deliverance, service* (in addition to the gift of *helps*), and *leading worship* (p. 11). See also Wagner's *Discover Your Spiritual Gifts, Updated and Expanded* (Regal Books, 2002, 2005).

- **23 gifts** – Bruce Bugabee, *Discover Your Spiritual Gifts the Network Way* (Zondervan, 2005). Bugabee includes four more gifts like *craftsmanship* and *creative communication* (p. 59), plus *hospitality* and *intercession* (p. 60).

- **20 gifts** – Jane A. G. Kise, David Stark, and Sandra Krebs Hirsh, *Lifekeys: Discover Who You Are, Revised Edition* (Bethany House, 1996, 2005). This book includes the additional gift of *hospitality* (pp. 88-90).

- **20 gifts** – Erik Rees, *S.H.A.P.E.: Finding and Fulfilling Your Unique Purpose for Life* (Zondervan, 2006) includes the additional gift of *hospitality* (p. 41).

- **20 gifts** – Kenneth Cain Kinghorn, *Discovering Your Spiritual Gifts* (Zondervan, 1981) also distinguishes between the gift of *helps* (p. 12) and *serving* (p. 13) to total 20.

I feel best about the last total and the finely threaded distinction that Kinghorn makes between *helps* and *serving*. I'm okay with the other two totals that include *hospitality* to reach a total of 20, although I don't think it can be fully justified biblically. But I feel a bit uneasy with the additional "gifts" to reach the totals of 23 and 27 because of their very pragmatic nature. It seems rather arbitrary to put these "gifts" alongside those that are mentioned in Scripture. Again, I think we can explain these additional ministries by appealing to gift-combinations without having to add "gifts" that aren't mentioned in the biblical lists. It is really an issue of determining which side you want to err on if you are wrong in your interpretation. Would I rather miss something in God's Word by being too cautious or would I prefer to add to what God has revealed to us in Scripture? I've chosen the former.

However, please allow me to balance my caution in limiting my discussion to 19 grace-gifts and make some allowance for the possibility that I could be wrong. I want to appeal to the Apostle Peter's statement about the richness of the grace-gifts we have received. He says this in 1 Peter 4:10: "As each one has received a special gift, employ it in serving one another as good stewards of *the manifold grace of God*" (my emphasis).

The Greek for *manifold* is *poikilos*. In this context *manifold* has nothing to do with the engine of your car and everything to do with the fact that there are "all kinds of" the grace of God. His grace is astonishingly varied. It is *manifold*. Far be it for me or anyone else to unduly limit the richness of the great diversity in His grace gifting of us while perhaps trying to be overly precise.

THE CESSATIONIST UNDERSTANDING OF TEMPORARY AND PERMANENT GIFTS

- **Temporary** (nine gifts)
  - **Foundational:** Apostleship, Prophesying, Word of Knowledge, Word of Wisdom

- o **Confirmatory:** Miracles, Healing, Tongues, Interpreting of Tongues and Discerning of spirits
- **Permanent** (ten gifts)
  - o Faith, Teaching, Helps/Serving, Mercy, Evangelizing, Pastor-Teacher, Leading/Ruling, Administrations, Giving and Exhortation

For more discussion of this issue, please see Appendix #1.

CONCLUSION

We are just beginning to see the diversity of the ministries that the saints can generate with the 19 grace-gifts and the numerous gift-combinations that can arise. It is absolutely staggering to think of the quality and volume of ministries that could erupt if we grew the church's ministry around these grace-gifted sheep and not just around their shepherds. Of course, the Devil knows this far better than we do and that is why he has thwarted the every-member-ministry from very early in the church's history (AD 110). The shift from seeing the church *as an organism* to seeing it *as an institution* started by building "the ministry" primarily around the ordained leadership offices. This shift and the 1,900 years of tradition that has reinforced it are deadly to the New Testament doctrine of the priesthood of all believers. This great truth is not to be "mystical mush" in our mouths, but it is to be incarnated in *a philosophy of ministry* that organically flows out of an all-believer-priesthood. Doing so will transform the non-organic church into *the organic, sustainable church.*

The second half of this chapter wrestled with the six somewhat formal lists of grace-gifts and the four very casual listings. We have at least 19 of these grace-gifts and a dizzying number of combinations for those believers who have more than one gift.

There is a sense in which the listing of these gifts/ministries raises their importance to a more noticeable level. This is why it is so amazing to me that I did not know about them my first ten years as a believer in Jesus and that the vast majority of God's people (80-90%) have so little experience with them personally. This is why we must study these gifts and teach them to new (and used) believers. Having the grace-gifts that we do is a very important part of our present experience of God's grace in our lives. It is God's serving grace that flows in an unending and commingled torrent with His saving grace. That's why His grace is what it is—*manifold*. Such manifold grace is the foundation of *the sustainable church*.

Chapter Seven

GROWING MINISTRY AROUND THE GRACE-GIFTS OF THE SAINTS

....

As I'm sitting at my desk in my home office trying to write this chapter, I'm taking a break and reading our local newspaper (remember them?). It is the week before Easter and various churches are advertising their holiday services. Page five is a full-page color ad for a new "granddaughter" church that recently came out of a daughter church that split off from the mother church in our city. Did you get that? On page seven is a half-page color ad of the daughter church that split from the mother church eight years ago. On page 11 is another full-page ad of a *second* daughter church that very recently split from the same mother church. One needs a scorecard to keep track of the spiritual divorces that have fractured the body of Christ in our community.

Having some inside information about each of these three churches reveals a common thread: the reason each started was so that a pastor could continue preaching after he was let go by his previous church. The specific rationale for one of them was "Because I want to or have to continue to preach." A second explanation was "As a fired pastor, I have to have a job." Note that these are less than robust biblical rationales for one church involuntarily spawning another church when a pastor is dismissed. However, our faulty assumption that the church builds her ministry around the shepherd's gifts, not the sheep's, so thoroughly stupefies us that we don't even bat an eye at such unhealthy pastor-centric beginnings.

This is just one of many reasons why we need to continue the discussion of how the New Testament grows the ministry or service of the church around the grace-gifts of the sheep, not the shepherds. This is a fundamental distinction between the non-organic church and the organic church. We cannot transform the non-organic church and enjoy the fullness of the organic, sustainable church without embracing this difference between the two. To accomplish this we must answer seven important questions about Christ's gifting of us.

ANSWERING SEVEN CRUCIAL QUESTIONS ABOUT GRACE-GIFTS

1. What is a "grace-gift" or "spiritual gift"?

It is a supernatural ability given by God to every Christian so that he or she can minister to others.[1] It is a God-given endowment that is *spiritual* by nature (Greek, *pneumatikos* in 1 Cor. 12:1, 14:1). It is more than a spiritual responsibility; rather, it is an ability *to serve/minister* in a spiritual manner. It is also more than a natural talent, although it usually corresponds quite nicely to these innate, God-given abilities. Grace-gifts are a continuing dimension of God's grace in our lives. They build upon *God's saving grace* and are part of *His serving grace*. Unfortunately, so many Christians only experience His saving grace and are unaware of God's *serving* grace. The fuller story is that we are saved by God's grace and we are also enabled to serve by His grace.

2. Who distributes the grace gifts?

This may sound like a very easy question, but the answer is actually a bit more profound than you may think. This is because the answer is Trinitarian:

- *The Father* is *the source* of our grace gifts; they are *from* Him (Rom. 12:3)

- The gifts are *given by the Son* in His role as the triumphant and glorified Messiah (Eph. 4:7-11)

- The ascended Christ gives them *through the Holy Spirit* and according to the Spirit's will (1 Cor. 12:8-11)

Our grace gifts are given *from the Father, by the Son, through the Holy Spirit*. When we ignore this amazing expression of His grace, we are ignoring the work of the triune God. Both God's saving grace and His serving grace are Trinitarian in nature.

3. Who gets the grace gifts?

They are only given to God's children—those who have been born into God's family by His saving grace through faith in Jesus Christ. Four times the statement is made that these continuing expressions of God's serving grace were then given *to each one of us* (1 Cor. 12:7, 11; Eph. 4:7; 1 Pet. 4:10). Please note these five important facts about your grace-gift(s):

1. You have at least one gift that defines your role in the body of Christ, i.e., your "body part" (1 Cor. 12:7, 11; Eph. 4:16).

2. You may have more than one gift; most Christians likely have at least two.

3. You do not have all of the gifts (1 Cor. 12:29-31).

4. Each and every gift is needed to be a complete body (1 Cor. 12:14-18).

5. Your developing of your gifts will likely determine your capacity for service/ministry (see Rom. 12:6-8).

4. When are the gifts given?

None of the four central passages about grace-gifts answers this explicitly, though it is *implied* in three of the passages. In my understanding of Scripture, it is at the moment of saving faith/conversion, when we are baptized with the Holy Spirit, that we are given our grace-gift(s):

> [11]But one and the same Spirit works all these things, distributing to each one individually just as He wills. [12]For even as the body is one and yet has many members, and all the members of the body, though they are many are one body, so also is Christ. [13]For by one Spirit we were all baptized into one body, whether Jews or Greeks, whether slaves or free, and we were all made to drink of one Spirit (1 Cor. 12:11-13; compare Rom. 12:4-6).

1 Corinthians 14:23 also implies that salvation and the giving of the grace-gifts are simultaneous because "ungifted persons" are *unbelievers*. The bottom line is that when we were baptized with the Holy Spirit by Jesus, we received our grace-gift(s).

However, some Christians read 1 Corinthians 12:31a—"But earnestly desire the greater gifts"—and reach a different conclusion. They argue that since we should desire greater grace gifts *after we become a Christian*, then the giving of the gifts is open-ended and not limited to the time of our conversion. There are three important clarifications that will help resolve this issue. First, Paul's use of the phrase "greater gifts" is not a devaluing of the worth of some of the gifts in relation to others. Paul has been making the *opposite* point in 1 Corinthians 12:14-26. Rather, a gift's "greatness quotient" *in this context* is related to its ability to edify others in the assembly. This is one reason why the "understood *you*"who should earnestly desire the greater gifts in 12:31a is a plural *you*—"you all." You Corinthians, as a whole church, should earnestly desire to use the more edifying gifts when the church assembles (e.g., 1 Cor. 14:26).

Second, with this exhortation to desire greater gifts, Paul is announcing his next topic, which he will unpack in 1 Corinthians 14. Note how 1 Corinthians 14:1 resumes this topic. In other words, 1 Corinthians 12:31 looks forward in terms of Paul's theme rather than backward in a summarizing manner. But before Paul explains the greater edification of prophecy over tongues in Chapter Fourteen, he says in 12:31b, "And I show you a still more excellent way." This announces the intervening topic in Chapter Thirteen: the more excellent and enduring way is loving one another, rather than overemphasizing grace gifts. This is the third clarification to the issue of earnestly desiring greater grace gifts. In the context of 1 Corinthians 12-14, Paul's statement is certainly not about seeking higher status through desiring, praying for, and then getting a "greater gift" from the Lord. Rather, all three chapters are about maximally edifying one another when the church gathers for her assembly.

Paul's exhortation to "earnestly desire the greater gifts" in 1 Corinthians 12:31a is not an encouragement to each of us as individual believers to desire to "upgrade" from the grace gifts we were given at salvation. Nor does it have anything to say about the giving of grace-gifts being open-ended. Rather, we are to delight in and enjoy what the Holy Spirit has already given us: "But one and the same Spirit works all these things, *distributing to each one individually just as He wills*" (1 Cor. 12:11; my emphasis).

An important point of application regarding when the gifts are given has to do with the amount of time we may waste between when we receive our gifts and when we begin to discover and use them. I wasted my first 10-12 years as a believer, unaware that grace-gifts existed, let alone that I had some of them. This is one reason why I am motivated to educate other believers about the astonishing resources of God's serving grace. This is my prayer for you:

> Oh Lord, please enable this dear reader to redeem the time that she or he has left to use her/his gifts to your greatest glory. I would also be so bold to ask if You would add grace-on-top-of-grace and help her/him to compensate for the time that has been lost. I ask this in the name of Jesus, the giver of our gifts. Amen.

5. What is the basis for the giving of the gifts?

It has nothing to do with our merit but everything to do with God's grace. This is why the primary term used to refer to our gifts is not *spiritual gifts* (Greek, *pneumatikos*), but *grace-gifts* (Greek, *charisma* in Rom. 12:6; 1 Cor. 12:4, 9, 28, 30, 31; and 1 Pet. 4:10).[2]

If the basis for the giving of our grace-gifts is the pouring out of God's serving grace when we entered the body of Christ, then we need to realize that it has nothing to do with our merit or our prayers, spiritual maturity, desires, etc. Not once, but four times in 1 Corinthians 12:8-11 Paul says that our grace-gifts were given by or through the Holy Spirit (vv. 8-10) and that He distributed them "to each one individually just as He wills" (v. 11).

I can say without exaggeration that it has taken me over forty years to come to grips with the fact that I do not have the grace gift of *leadership*, but I have the gift of *pastor-teacher*. Don't be a "wannabe" for gifts you don't have. I say this with great sadness from my own experience. You will waste an enormous amount of physical and emotional energy trying to be an organic part the body *that you are not* and this will only frustrate the process of you settling into the part of the body *that you are*. Instead, listen to and believe the consistent feedback you receive from the body of Christ about your grace gifting (see Rom. 12:3-8). There will be great freedom, joy and fruitfulness when you simply start being who you really are in the body.

6. Why are the gifts given—for what purpose?

The Apostle Paul could not answer this any more pointedly than he does in 1 Corinthians 12:7: "But to each one is given the manifestation of the Spirit *for the common good*" (my emphasis). Paul restates this purpose in 14:12: "So also you, since you are zealous of spiritual gifts, seek to abound *for the edification of the church*" (my emphasis). Grace-gifts were given to *each of us* for the good of *all of us* in the body of Christ. And as we selflessly build up one another, there is an astonishing overflow to the world's many people groups. This, in fact, is the specified purpose for the four gifts of apostles, prophets, evangelists and pastor-teachers in Ephesians 4:11. They edify the church specifically by "the equipping of the saints for the work of service, *to the building up of the body of Christ*" (Eph. 4:12; my emphasis).

Edifying ourselves is not the primary purpose of our grace-gifts. However, personal edification is nonetheless *a by-product* of using our gifts. Paul makes this point when discussing the gift of tongues in the assembly: "One who speaks in a tongue *edifies himself*, but one who prophesies edifies the church" (1 Cor. 14:4; my emphasis). There is nothing inherently evil about edifying ourselves when we use our grace-gifts. It is just a secondary effect—a by-product.

J. I. Packer enriches our understanding of the purpose of our gifts by relating them to the person of Christ:

> Gifts are manifestations of the Holy Spirit (1 Cor. 12:4-11) given to build up the church (12:7; 14:4) and the individuals within it. It is only through Christ, in Christ, and by learning and responding to Christ that anyone is edified. Therefore, gifts should be defined in terms of him—as powers of expressing, celebrating, displaying, and obeying Christ. Gifts communicate his reality through word or action in service of God and others (fellow believers and non-Christians too).[3]

Amazingly, as the Spirit-gifted body of Christ, we are given serving grace to continue the work of Christ. The grace-gifts we are given as believers function as Jesus' job description for our body part's specific contribution to *His on-going work* in and through His organic body.

On a pastoral note, God also graces us with the freedom to misuse and twist the power of our grace-gifts so that they have *a self-serving purpose.* Many of us have seen the confusing and unedifying impact from this kind of spiritual abuse in the church. Selfish, spotlight-grabbing use of grace-gifts often leads to unhealthy, dysfunctional attachments to leaders. Whole churches can become addicted to this type of person and their corresponding leadership style. This is why giftedness should never be substituted for character in the church's leaders. Better to have leaders with less eye-popping giftedness and godly character than supremely gifted leaders who redirect God's serving grace to their own ends. My observation is that God's people—and most people in general—readily trade character for giftedness the vast majority of the time.[4]

7. Why do different people with the same gift have different effects in ministry?

There are three parts to the answer to this question. First, listen to Paul's words on this topic in 1 Corinthians 12:4-6 (my emphasis):

[4]Now there are *varieties of gifts*, but the same Spirit.

[5]And there are *varieties of ministries*, and the same Lord.

[6]There are *varieties of effects*, but the same God who works all things in all persons.

Paul is saying that different effects are due to a sovereign God. He may choose to make some more effective and fruitful than others who have the same gift. Again, we bump up against that marvelous concept that He is God and we are not. Our goal is *to be faithful* in using our grace-gifts and trust that God will be just in rewarding us according to our faithfulness, not our fruitfulness. Focusing on the latter can be very misleading in the context of rewards. Jesus' Parable of the Talents in Matthew 25:14-30 makes this abundantly clear. The master rewards the servant who doubled his *five* talents with *exactly the same commendation* that he gave the servant who doubled his *two* talents: "Well done, good and faithful servant. You have been faithful over a little; I will set you over much. Enter into the joy of your master." (Matt. 25:21, 23; ESV). Comparing our abilities to those of another servant (Matt. 25:15) is to miss Jesus' point.

Paul speaks of his own gifts and ministry in 1 Corinthians 4:1 from the perspective of being *a servant* of Christ and *a steward* ["manager;" Greek, οἰκονόμος] of the mysteries of God that were revealed to him. He then ends his discussion with this well-known proverbial saying about servants/stewards: "Moreover, it is required of stewards, that one be found *faithful*" (1 Cor. 4:2; my translation and emphasis). *Be faithful.*

Secondly, we can also explain the different effects to some degree by appealing to the different life-settings, histories and self-educating efforts of those with the same grace-gifts. For example, two people have *the gift of faith*. One reads countless biographies of great saints from the past who had the gift of faith and gains great insight into how to believe God for unbelievable things. He also writes down the persons and things that he prays for and notes how God answered his prayers. He memorizes several key passages in the Bible about praying with faith, which he does every morning with his raggedy, yellowed prayer lists. All of these practices nurture his growth in his understanding of his gift and how to exercise it in a biblical manner.[5] The other person does not do any of these things. There will be an obvious difference in the effect of the same gifting between these two saints. Again, we come back to being faithful in both the use of our grace-gifts and in the development of our gifts. Our grace-gifts are like muscles that need to be exercised to grow and develop. No exercise, no growth. Different effects. *Be faithful.*

Lastly, we can explain the different effects by appealing to the different gift-combinations in each person's life. For example, two saints have *the gift of exhortation*. The first also has *the gift of teaching*. The combination of these two gifts helps this saint to become an amazingly clear teacher of God's Word who also applies it with penetrating sensitivity. This is the effect that you would expect with the gift-combination of *teaching + exhortation*. The second saint with the gift of exhortation also has *the gift of word of wisdom*. Both the gift of exhortation and the gift of word of wisdom are Bible-oriented gifts, but they both focus on *the application of God's Word*, not the explanation of it. Therefore, this saint was not created to be a great teacher of God's Word and should not feel inferior because he is not one. However, this gift-combination is phenomenal for counseling and providing spiritual guidance for God's people. This believer is perfect for this role in the body of Christ. He or she should be faithful in it.

One practical takeaway from this discussion is this: beware of patterning your ministry after another Christian. This is a recipe for envious comparison and either disappointment or pride. Rather, pattern your ministry after saints with any gift combination who are wonderfully *faithful* in the development and use of their gifts. This way you will be focusing on the one thing over which you have some control. God's choices affect *the fruitfulness* of our ministries (1 Cor. 12:4-6). Our choices affect *the faithfulness* of our ministries. It really boils down to a pretty simple formula. *Be faithful.*

CONCLUSION

In this chapter we explained a little more of the New Testament's organic, sustainable model of every-member ministry by answering seven crucial questions about grace-gifts. In the next chapter we will define and describe each of the 19 grace-gifts.

I hope that you are beginning to see how much dignity the Triune God deeds to the saints by entrusting the ongoing ministry of Messiah Jesus to us. The institutional model—the non-organic church—has undercut and diminished that dignity, producing a shriveled, shrunken view of the ministry of the saints that is not worthy of life on this side of the vacated cross and the empty tomb. Quite to the contrary, Jesus went through what He did in order to share His continuing ministry *with all of us.* One of the main purposes of Jesus pouring forth the Holy Spirit on Pentecost (Acts 2:33) was to empower *all of us to minister* (Acts 2:14-18).[6] Is that too good to be true? *No.* It is too true to be anything less.

Chapter Eight

NINETEEN EXPRESSIONS OF GOD'S SERVING GRACE

....

Our goal in this chapter is to describe each of the 19 grace-gifts and to explain the process of discovering the gifts that Jesus has given to each of His followers. However, describing each of the grace-gifts is not as simple as you may imagine. As someone who teaches both the New Testament and hermeneutics (how to interpret the Bible), I can attest that there is a boatload of interpretive issues that comes with defining and describing each grace-gift.

First, in the New Testament's longest discussion of the gifts in 1 Corinthians 12-14, Paul is correcting the Corinthians' abuse of grace-gifts, not laying out a fully orbed theology of them. His discussion is very specific to the Corinthians' historical context. Secondly, with several of the gifts, we are working with *a one-word context*. Add to that the third difficulty that several of the gifts are only mentioned *one time*. Pardon my bad English, but all of these *ones* lead to a lot of interpretive *funs*. Our overly precise interpretive conclusions may resemble more an interpretive funhouse rather than the household of God. Gordon Fee summarizes this well:

> All of this suggests not only that we do not have here [in 1 Cor. 12-14] a systematic discussion of "spiritual gifts," but also that there is some doubt as to whether the apostle himself had precise and

identifiably different "gifts" in mind when he wrote these words. In any case, he would almost certainly not recognize some of the schematizing that later interpreters have brought to these texts.[1]

Being one of those "later interpreters" who is now trying to "schematize" the biblical texts about grace-gifts, I will try not to go beyond the biblical data and conclude things that don't fit in with a biblical perspective. I will tell you when I am going beyond what the Bible says about a grace-gift. I will tell you when I am appealing to *my experience in the body of Christ with these various "gifts"*—which are *ministries*. While one's experience with these ministries/gifts is also a very important source of truth, it is not an inerrant, infallible source like the Bible.

DESCRIPTIONS OF EACH GRACE-GIFT

1. Apostles [Greek, *apostolos*] (1 Cor. 12:28-29; Eph. 4:11; compare Acts 1:21-26; Eph. 2:19-22; 1 Cor. 15:5-9; 2 Cor. 12:11-12)

Special Note: This gift is still being discussed as to whether it has ceased because it was a uniquely *foundational office* specifically for the beginning of the church (Eph. 2:19-20; cf. 2 Cor. 12:12) or if it is a presently given *grace-gift*. I am not exaggerating to say that we will probably spend another 20 years or more debating this issue at the scholarly level. In the meantime, here is a helpful summary of the New Testament data about *apostles*:

> There are three kinds of apostles mentioned in the NT: those who had been with Jesus in his ministry and had witnessed his resurrection (Acts 1:21-22); Paul, who was born out of season (1 Cor. 15:8-9); and those who received the gift of apostleship. The first two categories are to be regarded as *offices*, whereas the last is *a spiritual gift to the church*. In the present context [Eph. 4:11] *the apostle* refers to the third kind, *the gift of apostle*.[2]

Jesus' twelve apostles and Paul fill *the foundational office of apostle*. In addition to them, the following persons are also called *apostles* in the New Testament:

> To mention some, we cite Barnabas (Acts 14:4, 14; 1 Cor. 9:5-7), James, the Lord's brother (1 Cor. 15:7; Gal. 1:19), Apollos (1 Cor. 4:6, 9), probably Silvanus (1 Thess. 2:6 [GT 2:7]), Titus (2 Cor. 8:23), Epaphroditus (Phil. 2:25), and possibly Andronicus and Junia[s] (Rom. 16:7). *These had the gift of apostleship.*[3]

If this summary is accurate, and I think it is, then we do not have to see apostles as either an office or a grace gifting. Rather than *either/or*, it is *both/and*. The New Testament appears to use *apostle* for *both* the initial establishing office of the twelve and Paul—part of the foundation of the church (Eph. 2:19-20)—*and* for those who follow them in similar and analogous type ministries *as grace-gifted apostles*. This latter group of apostles is now being fitted together in "the whole building/holy temple" of the church (Eph. 2:21-22) that rests upon the foundation of the apostles and prophets and Jesus, the cornerstone (2:19-20).

All of this is to say that I can now give a *provisional* definition of the grace-gift of *apostle*:

> **Apostleship (definition):** The special ability to initiate the work of the church in new areas or in new ways that provides extraordinary health, growth, and maturity through this leadership, thus fulfilling *its equipping function* (Eph. 4:11-12).

Here are two respected scholars who describe this gift in similar fashion:

Kenneth Klinghorn: "*Apostleship* is the ability to communicate the Christian message across cultural (and frequently linguistic) barriers and plant a Christian church where there is no knowledge of the gospel. The term in Greek (*apostolos*) and Latin (*missio*) means 'a sent one' or 'a messenger.' The rough modern equivalent is a pioneer missionary.[4]

Harold Hoehner: "It seems then that the main function of an apostle is to establish churches in areas that have not been reached by others (Rom. 15:20). They are God's messengers to open up new territories for Christ.[5]

2. Prophecy [Greek, *prophēteia*] (1 Cor. 12:10, 28-29; 13:2, 8; 14:all; Rom. 12:6; Eph. 4:11; compare Acts 13:1; 15:32; 21:8-9; 1 Thess. 5:19-22)

Special Note: There has been an intense scholarly discussion about this gift over the last 30 years as to whether or not it has ceased to be given. If it is still given, then the exact definition of "prophecy" has also been debated. The definitions have ranged from powerful preaching to foretelling the future. The definition given here reflects the basic consensus. *Prophecy* is mentioned more than any other grace-gift. It is in all seven gift lists in 1 Corinthians 12-14 and in the Romans 12 and Ephesians 4:11 gift lists. For those who are skeptical of prophecy or have never experienced it, it may be helpful to note what Paul says about this gift in 1 Thessalonians 5:19-22: "Do not quench the Spirit; do not despise prophetic utterances. But examine everything carefully; hold fast to that which is good; abstain from every form of evil."

> **Prophecy (definition):** The ability to transmit spontaneous, Spirit-given, intelligible messages, usually spoken in the gathered church, for the edification, encouragement and consolation of the people (1 Cor. 14:3). Prophets likely *equip the saints* (Eph. 4:11-12) by calling the church back to biblical values and appropriate emphases that insure the body's wisest and most fruitful ministry.

3. Teaching [Greek, *didaskalia*] (1 Cor. 12:28-29; 1 Cor. 14:6, 26; Rom. 12:7)

Teaching (definition): The keen interest in the personal study of God's Word and the capacity to communicate clearly the truths and applications of the Word so others may learn and profit.

Those with the gift of teaching love to get lost in the wonders of the biblical text and hop down all of the interesting "bunny trails" that intersect with the passage they are studying. Spirit-gifted teachers also love books. Their *strength* is in the study and understanding of the Bible—the first half of the communication process. Teachers seek to help God's people *to understand* what God has revealed. Their *need for discipline* is in the back half of the communication process—the life-related packaging of the biblical truth for God's people. In this respect *teachers and exhorters* are the mirror-opposite of one another in their strengths and needs for self-discipline.

4. Helps/Serving [*helps* (Greek, *antilēmpsyis*) in 1 Cor. 12:28 and *serving/ministering* (Greek, *diakonia*) in Rom 12:7]

Helps/Serving (definition): The unusual capacity to serve faithfully in practical ways by taking care of material needs and "household duties" in the Lord's work so that others are encouraged and strengthened spiritually.

Special Note: Douglas Moo makes this observation about using the Greek word *diakonia* for the specific grace-gift of *serving* when it was already used as the general word for all Christian ministry:

> Paul never elsewhere mentions "service" as a distinct gift, and some commentators think therefore that he uses it very generally here, of any kind of ministry that a Christian might have. But the other gifts in these verses [Rom. 12:6-8] involve specific functions. Probably, then, Paul thinks of a specific gift of service that qualifies a person to fill the office of "deacon," a ministry that apparently involved especially organizing and providing for

the material needs of the church.... The gift of "service" should not become an occasion of pride (v. 3) but should be the foundation for heartfelt and sacrificial "serving" of others.[6]

In 1 Corinthians 12:28, the word "helps" appears to have the added connotation of helping the weak, needy and poor. The interpretive issue with this gift is whether or not Paul is using *helps* and *serving* as synonymous terms in 1 Corinthians and Romans (my view) or if there is a subtle difference between these two ministries/gifts (Kinghorn).[7]

5. Mercy [Greek, *eleos*] (Rom. 12:8)

Mercy (definition): The capacity to connect emotionally with the hurting and to give undeserved, compassionate aid, especially to those whom the majority ignores. Those with this gift should exercise it cheerfully (Rom 12:8).

The fact that many of us in the body of Christ are drawn to attractive, popular people is offset by those with the gift of mercy. These dear saints see the hurting, the maladjusted, the troubled, the unlovely, those scarred by sin and life's tragedies and are not put off by their emotional or physical brokenness. Think of how impoverished our ministry in Jesus' name would be without this lovely gift of compassion.

6. Evangelism [Greek, *euangelion*] (Eph. 4:11)

Evangelism (definition): The capacity and overwhelming burden to present the gospel message with exceptional clarity and to train others effectively to do so. This latter aspect fulfills *the equipping dimension* of this gift (Eph. 4:11) by sensitizing and shaping the body of Christ for "body evangelism" in its ongoing mission of incarnating and proclaiming the gospel of Jesus Christ.

An interesting fact about American Christianity is that the majority of evangelical schools have not been started by teachers, but by evangelists. This expresses the equipping function of this gift and is an overlooked aspect of it.

7. Pastor-Teacher [Greek, *poimēn didaskalos*] (Eph. 4:11)

> **Pastor-Teacher (definition):** The capacity to shepherd God's flock (feed, lead, and give heed to) and to prepare and serve a balanced spiritual diet that produces growth. As one of the four *equipping gifts*, this dimension is fulfilled when pastor-teachers create an environment and corresponding structures that help God's people to discover and develop their grace gifts.

Special Note: This is a grace *gift*, not an office. Therefore, it enables *both men and women* to serve in many capacities in the life of the church where the shepherding and biblical feeding of God's people is needed (e.g., ministries to children, youth, women, men, etc.).[8] On the Bible-teaching spectrum, where *teachers* are more content-oriented on one end and *exhorters* are more application-oriented on the other, *pastor-teachers* are in the middle with a dual focus on both content and shepherding/ application.

8. Leadership [Greek, *proistamenos* = the one who leads or gives aid] (Rom. 12:8)

> **Leadership (definition):** The capacity to stand *before* others to guide them and to catalyze God's people to action in a caring and concerned manner. This gift is to be exercised *with diligence* or *eagerness* (Rom. 12:8).

Special Note: The Greek word that is translated *the one who leads* in Romans 12:8 can mean "lead" or "be concerned about, care for, or give aid." *Leading* has a stronger connotation and *giving aid* has a softer, more relational texture. *Leading* is probably the better understanding in this context and likely points to those who serve as elders of a local congregation. This is supported by this term being used to refer to elders *who lead* well in

1 Timothy 5:17 and to the elders "who diligently labor among you, and *have charge over* you in the Lord and give you instruction" in 1 Thessalonians 5:12 (my emphasis).

This gift is not meant to be exercised in an autocratic, heavy-handed manner. Jesus' exhortation to His disciples about being *servant-leaders* (Mark 10:35-45/Matt. 20:20-28) makes this abundantly clear. Those with this gifting should lay awake at night and anticipate the next steps that God's people should take that will best express Jesus' concern for the body's well-being. Spirit-gifted leaders bring a confidence and direction to the church. Generally speaking, most Christian groups will struggle without someone having this grace-gift. My experience has been that most pastors think that they have this gift and most of the rest of us do not. While the grace-gift of *pastor-teacher* has a leadership aspect that overlaps somewhat with that of *leadership*, it relates more to the shepherding function rather than a pure leadership function. We will look more closely at the role of leadership in the church in Chapter Twelve.[9]

9. Administrations [Greek, *kubernēseis*] (1 Cor. 12:28)

> **Administrations (definition):** The capacity to stand *behind* others to guide them and to bring structure and organization to the church's work in an efficient and ordered way by delegating responsibilities to others.

Special Note: The distinction between this gift and *leadership* is the absence of the catalyzing function. Note that this gift is in the plural. It has a one word context that only occurs one time. This means that our *biblical* understanding of it is largely derived by the way the Greek word is used in extra-biblical contexts. For example, we appeal to its usage describing the steering of a ship. This is slender material. However, our *experiential* understanding of this gift is rich. I have closely observed someone with the gift of administrations for over 42 years—my wife Marty. She has the supernatural ability to bring order out of chaos. She knows what to do and how to delegate responsibilities to others to get it done. It is a marvelous, much-needed gift.

10. Giving [Greek, *metadidous* = the one who gives] (Rom. 12:8)

> **Giving (definition):** The capacity to distribute personal resources to the Lord's work and to His people in a very need-sensitive, consistent, generous, cheerful and sacrificial manner.

Paul instructs those with the gift of giving to exercise it with *simplicity* or singleness of heart and intention in Romans 12:8. The gift of giving is obvious in *its benefit* to the body of Christ, but secretive in *its expression* in light of Jesus' teaching on our manner of giving (Matt. 6:1-4). Many times those who have this gift also seem to have an ability to make money.

11. Faith [Greek, *pistis*] (1 Cor. 12:9; 13:2)

> **Faith (definition):** The capacity to trust God beyond the probable due to an extraordinary, Spirit-given confidence in God and His resources. The result is that the faith and vision of others in the body are raised and *their faith* is strengthened when this gift is expressed.

Just read the biographies of great saints like Francis of Assisi (1182-1226) or George Müller of Bristol (1805-1898) and you will see vivid expressions of the gift of faith in a believer's life. Those with this gift should definitely read the biographies of Christians who had this gift to build their own faith and to learn how others expressed this gift in their lives. Those with the gift of faith should be the backbone of the prayer and intercessory ministries of their church or parachurch ministry. It is not a vague, mushy spiritual gift, but an essential and strategic gifting that should be richly cultivated and expressed in the life of the church. *Faith* is also immensely crucial in terms of spiritual warfare. It is the fourth of six pieces of "the full armor of God" in Ephesians 6:10-17: "in addition to all, taking up *the shield of faith* with which you will be able to extinguish all the flaming arrows of the evil one" (Eph. 6:16; my emphasis).

12. Exhortation [Greek, *parakalōn* = the one who exhorts] (Rom. 12:8)

> **Exhortation (definition):** The capacity to encourage, comfort and motivate people to action using God's Word. (See Barnabas in Acts 4:36-37 and 11:22-24 as an example of someone with this gift.)

Special Note: There is a range of meaning for the Greek word translated as *exhorter*. It includes the functions of *encouraging* and *comforting*. Therefore, it is likely that this gift has a range of applications from motivating to encouraging to comforting.

Exhorters love to take God's Word and apply it vigorously to people's lives. They are marvelous at illustrating the truth and making it vivid. While their strength is on the applicational end of the communication process, their need for discipline is on the study end of the process. Exhorters can be so anxious to move to the application of the Word that they may be too brief in the study and interpretation of a passage. They will need to discipline themselves to spend a bit more time going deeper into interpreting the meaning of the passage. This will pay off with greater spiritual power in the applications that they discover.

Exhortation joins *teaching* and *pastor-teacher* as the three *Bible-oriented* grace-gifts we have observed up to this point. Perhaps it will be helpful to lay out these three ministries on a spectrum that compares them according to their interest in depth-of-study versus relevance-in-application:

EXHORTATION	PASTOR-TEACHER	TEACHING
▲	▲	▲
Interest in the *relevance* of the truth	Dual focus on both biblical content and the flock's needs	Interest in the *understanding* of the truth

The next two grace-gifts—*a word of wisdom and a word of knowledge*—are *Bible-oriented* grace-gifts like exhortation, pastor-teacher and teaching. We can now add these two Bible-centered gifts to complete our Bible-oriented spectrum of spiritual gifts:

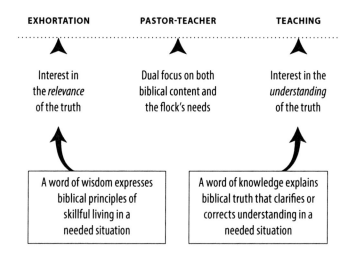

13. **A Word of Wisdom** [Greek, *logos sophias*] (1 Cor. 12:8)

Word of Wisdom (definition): The special capacity to value and glean God's wisdom from the Scriptures and to apply it to life situations. God's children desperately need *His* word of wisdom at crucial junctures through this gift to direct or correct their path so that they may be wise—i.e., skillful in living—in a wide variety of circumstances.

A word of wisdom is not revealed directly from the Spirit on the spot, but rather is the sensitivity to the Spirit in the apprehension of wise principles gleaned from the study of the Scripture over time. However, *the expression* of this biblical wisdom accumulated over time may be *in the moment* on many occasions as the need for God's wisdom arises. To sense this need, those saints with this ministry usually have *greater discernment of others' issues*. They discern a saint's needs and then meet them with a wise word from God that was gleaned from the study of His Word. Perhaps this helps explain why the one mention of this grace-gift is in the indefinite singular: "*a* word of wisdom." This indefinite singular expression may also help explain the next gift: "*a* word of knowledge." Both ministries may involve the imparting of *a timely word* to meet the need of the moment within the body of Christ.

Special Note: This gift is mentioned one time (1 Cor. 12:8). The major interpretive questions are the same regarding the nature of *a word of wisdom* and *a word of knowledge*:

- Are these two gifts *of a more miraculous nature*—instantaneous and revelatory words of wisdom and knowledge directly from the Holy Spirit? Or are they *non-miraculous*, Bible-oriented gifts where the gifted believer is supernaturally enabled to gain the wisdom or knowledge over time through the study of God's Word?

- The *more miraculous* interpretation is widely held by most in Pentecostal, charismatic and Third Wave churches. The *non-miraculous* is held by a minority in those churches and by the majority of evangelicals outside of those theological circles who have an opinion on this matter.

I lean toward *the non-miraculous understanding* as the correct one for both gifts due to the nature of both wisdom and knowledge in the Bible and especially in Corinth (1 Cor. 1:18-2:16).[10] Additionally, the instantaneous and revelatory words of wisdom and knowledge that are directly from the Holy Spirit are actually *prophetic utterances* and should be guided by the rich biblical guidelines that are given for *prophecy* (e.g., 1 Cor. 14 and 1 Thess. 5:19-22). There is no need to have additional gifts when these needs are *fully met* with the gift of prophecy. Moreover, we recover specific gifts that are Bible-oriented when we go this direction. See the very helpful summary by Wayne Grudem that supports this particular interpretation.[11]

14. A Word of Knowledge [Greek, *logos ginōseōs*] (1 Cor. 12:8; compare 1 Cor. 13:2, 8; 14:6)

> **Word of Knowledge (definition):** This is very similar to, or actually another way of describing, the gift of **teaching**. If it is a separate grace-gift, it may be the ability to impart biblical knowledge about God, His grace and His plan, etc. to meet an immediate need. While the biblical knowledge is gleaned over time, through the careful study of God's Word, this ministry may be expressed *in the moment* to clarify or correct an immediate need or concern about biblical truth.

Special Note: As I mentioned in the previous discussion about a word of wisdom, this gift is *not* receiving new facts/knowledge directly from the Spirit about a situation or person; that is *prophecy*. Rather, since knowledge is so very important in both the Bible and in the Greco-Roman culture, Paul may well be reclaiming its biblical basis for the Corinthian church:

> The same may be noted of the word *knowledge*. In 1 Corinthians 8:1-4, 7, 10 *knowledge* appears four times (see also 13:2, 8). Knowledge, according to Paul, is insight into the unfathomable depths of God's gracious work in Christ. Thus *the word of knowledge* may be "the special ability to put into words divinely revealed knowledge about God's grace."[12]

15. Distinguishing between Spirits [Greek, *diakriseis pneumatōn*] (1 Cor. 12:10)

> **Distinguishing between spirits (definition):** The capacity to distinguish between spirits of truth and error (Holy Spirit versus human and evil spirits) and to discern subtle forms of spiritual phoniness, especially in prophecies (1 Cor. 14:12, 14, 29 and 32).

1 John 4:1-6 is the New Testament's main exhortation to God's people to test and distinguish between spirits of truth and error. Note how the Apostle John orients us to this crucial issue: "Beloved, do not believe every spirit, but test the spirits to see whether they are from God, because many false prophets have gone out into the world" (1 John 4:1).

This gift is simply Jesus' empowering of some in His body with much greater sensitivity to and discernment of the spirit world. These Spirit-gifted saints should help lead the way in "testing the spirits" in order to protect the church. It may even include the ability to distinguish between various types of evil spirits.[13]

A word of encouragement is needed for those of you who have this gift, who have likely felt very strange as a believer in Jesus Christ most of your life. This is because you are perceiving spiritual things (spirit persons) that other Christians are not. In fact, most Christians in the Western world are naïve about and largely oblivious to the spirit world. Of course, this is part of the deception, as the seasoned demon Screwtape instructed novice demon Wormwood:

> I do not think you will have much difficulty in keeping the patient in the dark. The fact that 'devils' are predominantly *comic* figures in the modern imagination will help you. If any faint suspicion of your existence begins to arise in his mind, suggest to him a picture of something in red tights, and persuade him that since he cannot believe in that (it is an old

textbook method of confusing them), he therefore cannot believe in you.[14]

So, dear saints with this ministry, this is not your problem. You are not the one who is out-of-step with the world. It is those of us who are foolishly materialistic and naturalistic. You are perceiving the world as it really is. So, fulfill your ministry within the body of Christ until the rest of us catch up to you.[15]

My wife and I once knew a couple who had several children. The father was a very slick talker and an elder in his local church. Unfortunately, he was essentially an arrogant and narcissistic spiritual phony and was totally different at home with his children and his wife than he was at church. Moreover, he was involved in extra-marital affairs and was a threatening bully to his family. However, because he was a leader in the church, the rest of the church leaders believed his side of the story when he wanted to drive his wife out of the marriage and alienate her from the children. She ended up having to leave the home for her own safety. Additionally, the children were convinced by their father that their mother was the problem.

What was the outcome of this situation? The husband went on to have several failed marriages and, of course, readily gave up his phony faith in Christ. All of the children were terribly scarred by his sin and the fact that he eventually deserted them for another family he gained from a third or fourth marriage. Most of the children were alienated from their mother for years and they all left the Christian faith. One of them lived an especially rebellious life and was killed before age 20 in a drug-deal gone bad. The others simply walked away from Jesus and the people of God out of disdain for what they had seen.

Could this situation have ended differently? Quite possibly if there had been at least one or two saints in the church who had cultivated their grace-gifting of distinguishing between spirits. These saints could have discerned the husband/father's spiritual phoniness and could have persuaded the elders of the local church to look below the surface of this deceptive man's appearance. This much-needed functioning gift could have saved the teenager's life and the souls of the other bruised children. When we build ministry primarily around vocational shepherds and ignore the diverse gifting of the sheep, the cost in human suffering and spiritual heartache is great indeed.[16]

16. Workings of Mighty Powers/Miracles [Greek, *energēmata dunameōn* = workings of mighty powers or miracles] (1 Cor. 12:10, 28, & 29)

> **Workings of Mighty Power or Miracles (definition):** The capacity to perform acts contrary to natural laws with God's mighty power, which demonstrates His authoritative presence, especially in the gospel.

Special Note: The double plurals "workings of mighty powers/miracles" may signify various kinds/times for this gift. It is also listed as a grace-gift three times along with, yet distinct from *gifts of healings* (1 Cor. 12:9-10, 28 and 29-30). Apparently, these miracles are in addition to physical healings. These workings of mighty powers may include deliverance from physical danger (Acts 5:19-26; 12:6-11), powerful works of judgment on enemies of the gospel or those who require church discipline (Acts 5:1-11; 13:9-12), miraculous deliverance from injury (Acts 28:3-6) or even triumph over demonic opposition (Acts 16:18; cf. Luke 10:17).[17]

17. Gifts of Healings [Greek, *charismata iamatōn*] (1 Cor. 12:9, 28-30)

Gifts of Healings (definition): The capacities to heal diseases miraculously. Perhaps this gifting includes being able to discern how to pray for healings that are specific to different kinds of needs.

Special Note: The plural form of the words "gifts" and "healings" *may* indicate that this is an ability that is given repeatedly—perhaps at special times, rather than on-demand.[18]

18. Speaking in Tongues [Greek, *genē glōssōn* = kinds of languages or tongues in 1 Cor. 12:10, 28, & Greek, *glōssais lalousin* = speak with languages or tongues in 1 Cor. 12:30] (See also 1 Cor. 13:1, 8; 14:all)

Speaking in Tongues (definition): The capacity to speak to God or to His people in praise or prayer in an unlearned *known* language (e.g., Acts 2:1-13) or an *unknown* language (e.g., 1 Cor. 14). Both are unlearned and not understood by the speaker. Speaking in tongues/languages should not be forbidden, but should be orderly and the languages interpreted in the assembly as a part of public praise and prayer (1 Cor. 14:39-40).

Special Note: Because the Corinthians abused this gift, Paul clarified that it is "the least" of the gifts (1 Cor. 12:28), it is not for all (12:30) and it should not be compared to "the greater gifts" (12:31). This evaluation is in light of the low "edification quotient" of speaking in tongues in the assembly without an interpreter. While I was taught and believed otherwise, it seems inescapable that tongues in 1 Cor. 14 are unknown languages that no one would understand without the spiritual gift of interpreting tongues.[19]

19. Interpreting Tongues [Greek, *hermēneia glōssōn* = interpretation of tongues] (1 Cor. 12:10, 30)

Interpreting Tongues (definition): The capacity to interpret the meaning of a tongue, although the interpreter has not learned the language or it is an unknown language.

CONCLUSION

I hope that you are as amazed as I am at the end of this panoramic survey of the grace-gifts that Jesus has given *to each one of us*. In writing about each of the grace-gifts, a question kept elbowing its way into my thoughts: *How much did it cost Jesus to give us our grace-gifts?* Paul devotes a whole paragraph in Ephesians to this question. What did our grace-gifts cost Jesus? His incarnation (Eph. 4:7-10):

> [7]But to each one of us grace was given according to the measure of Christ's gift. [8]Therefore it says, "WHEN HE ASCENDED ON HIGH, HE LED CAPTIVE A HOST OF CAPTIVES, AND HE GAVE GIFTS TO MEN AND WOMEN." [9]Now this expression, "He ascended," what does it mean except that He also had descended into the lower parts, that is the earth? [10]He who descended is Himself also He who ascended far above all the heavens, so that He might fill all things (my translation).

We tend to think of the necessity of Jesus' incarnation solely in terms of His need for a fully human body so that He could sacrifice Himself and thereby atone for our sins. This is absolutely true but absolutely *partial*. We are used to focusing on Jesus' incarnation only in terms of *God's saving grace*. True, but incomplete.

In Ephesians 4:7-10, Paul adds another reason for Jesus' incarnation: *dispensing God's serving grace*. The outpouring of God's grace does not stop at the atonement but continues throughout our whole time on earth, throughout the intermediate state and throughout all eternity. This *serving grace* is majestic, astonishingly diversified (manifold) and totally undeserved. It is grace from an overwhelmingly gracious Triune God. If you are reading this book, you have apparently responded to God's saving grace. But will you now embrace His serving grace by discovering and growing in your grace-gifts? Will you help other believers to do the same? We are designed to be the most dynamic organism in the world, a body that sustains *His* ministry until He returns. However, in the absence of focusing on the saints discovering and using their grace-gifts, we undermine the church's sustainability. May God help us to repent of our arrogant self-reliance and begin to live out His design for us as the body of Christ.

Chapter Nine

HOW WE DISCOVER THE SERVING GRACE OF GOD

· · · · · · · · · · · · · · · · · · · ·

"If highschoolers, housewives, working men and business women were to head out each day, not to school or housework or place of business, but to the ministry for which the Holy Spirit had equipped them, would not this help to make the day's employment purposeful, zestful and abundant?"

–Leslie B. Flynn[1]

Names are really significant in the Bible. Often they reveal the sense William McRae, in his excellent book, *The Dynamics of Spiritual Gifts*, suggests *five basic steps* to discover our grace-gifts.[2] I would modify this slightly by suggesting that these "steps" actually function as "aspects" of a less linear process that is far more dynamic and flexible:

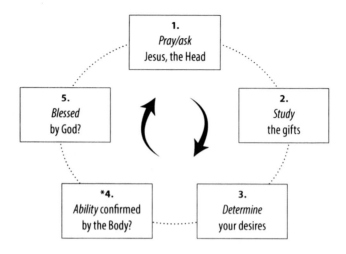

1. Begin by praying/asking Jesus, the head of the body.

Avoid anxiety due to your past inability to determine your gift(s) by talking to the Head of the body about His chosen function for you in His church. He wants you to discover your gifts far more than you want to discover them. So, ask Him to show you. Ask Him to reveal it to you as you study the grace-gifts in the New Testament, as you ponder your desires, as you glean feedback about your gifts from other members of the body and as you determine God's blessings of your efforts. These are the next four aspects you will go through and they will probably not be in a strict linear order. In many ways they are more circular and cyclical. You'll be taking the "steps" simultaneously or in different order. Likely, you won't find your gifts; your gifts will find you.[3]

2. Study the grace-gifts in the New Testament.

Study the biblical passages relating to grace gifts: Romans 12:3-8; Ephesians 4:11-12; 1 Peter 4:10-11; 1 Corinthians 12:6-10; 12:28; 12:29-30; 13:1-3; 13:8; 14:6; 14:26. Seek to understand each gift so you have a framework in which to ponder your own gifts. It's hard to know what you've found if you don't know what you were looking for. A little biblical information about the gifts goes a very long way in the discovery process. By the way, if you just picked this book up and started reading *this chapter first*, then you might want to ponder why you're taking such a pragmatic approach to living the Christian life. As followers of Christ, we need to know *what* something is and *why* it is important before we jump to *how to do it*.

Perhaps you might reply that *millions* of Christians throughout the history of the church did not even know that grace-gifts existed, yet they still fulfilled the ministries Jesus wanted them to have. I cannot disagree with that fact. However, the numbers tip the scales in favor of the other side of the argument. The harsh reality is that *tens of millions* of Christians throughout the history of the church and to this very hour have never had *the knowledge* that such things as grace-gifts even exist. They do not know that they have at least one grace-gift and that they have been empowered to minister on behalf of Christ through their gifting. If they would have been taught about grace-gifts or studied about them, they would have been far more likely to use and develop them. If they knew that they had been given a new Mercedes convertible, they would be far more likely to drive it than if they didn't know they been given such a gift. The Christian faith is a knowledge-based faith and generally we are to know before we do. Knowing our identity in Christ precedes and informs our action on behalf of Christ.

3. Determine what your desires are.

Based on the knowledge of your study of what the individual gifts are, what particular gifts strike a chord with you? What gifts would you desire to have because you find them most fulfilling as you use them or when you see others using them? Are you drawn to them because you desire the same gifts they are expressing? *What are your desires?*

If you are like I was for many years, I was not aware of *what I wanted to do*. Rather, I followed our family pattern of being very much aware *of what I ought to do*. While there are certainly many *oughts* in the Christian life, there are also a lot of *desires* that God appeals to in our lives because He placed them there. We have somehow embraced the false idea that being a Christian means being someone other than who I am and always doing things other than what I want to do. This is not to diminish the desperate need for our ugly, sinful desires to be transformed. It is simply to correct the distorted perspective that becoming like Jesus means denying and negating all of the lovely desires God sovereignly created in us. This is why it is important to monitor the things that we ponder as we lay awake at night. These falling-asleep-musings may give us great insight into things God has called us to do.

There is a passage written by Parker Palmer that speaks eloquently of being aware of our God-given calling and following these desires. I believe it's worth quoting at length:

> When we listen primarily for what we "ought" to be doing with our lives, we may find ourselves hounded by external expectations that can distort our identity and integrity. There is much that I ought to be doing by some abstract moral calculus. But is it my vocation? Am I gifted and called to do it? Is this particular ought a place of intersection between my inner self and the outer world, or is it someone else's image of how my life should look?
>
> When I only follow the oughts, I may find myself doing work that is ethically laudable but not mine to do. A vocation that is not mine, no matter how externally valued, does violence to the self—in the precise sense that it *violates* my identity and

112

integrity on behalf of some abstract norm. When I violate myself, I invariably end up violating the people I work with....

In contrast to the strained and even violent concept of vocation as an ought, Frederick Buechner offers a more generous and humane image of vocation as "the place where your deep gladness and the world's deep hunger meet."

In a culture that sometimes equates work with suffering, it is revolutionary to suggest that the best inward sign of vocation is deep gladness—revolutionary but true. If a work is mine to do, it will make me glad over the long haul, despite the difficult days. Even the difficult days will ultimately gladden me, because they pose the kinds of problems that can help me grow in a work if it is truly mine.

If a work does not gladden me in these ways, I need to consider laying it down. When I devote myself to something that does not flow from my identity, that is not integral to my nature, I am most likely deepening the world's hunger rather than helping to alleviate it.[4]

When we go about the seemingly innocuous task of determining what our desires are, we are actually going about the serious business of discovering *our calling in Christ* to the unique ministry that He has given each of us through our grace gifts. He wants us to become fully who He designed us to be in His body:

When it comes to mission, the most important resource any church has is the ministry calling of each of its members. But few churches are aware of that fact. Yes, somewhere in the church's purpose statement you may find the words, "every member a minister." But the way they "do church" makes it clear that they do not really believe their greatest asset is the ministry calling of the average person. Rather, they think their greatest assets are their pastor, facilities, location or perhaps their "style." In reality, however, the best thing your church has to offer is the good news of the gospel wrapped in the ministry calling of each of its people.[5]

*4. Have your ministry efforts resulted in recognized abilities that are confirmed by the body of Christ?

This means getting involved in ministry in your local church or Christian group and doing the things you desire to do. Try several different areas and types of ministry. Be experimental and take risks. Which area or areas manifest real abilities that others recognize in you? Are these abilities confirmed by the leaders/ elders/mature members of your local church? This process takes time, so don't get impatient.

I put a star by number four because this may be the most important part of the whole process. Discovering what our ministries are in the body of Christ is not something that we can do sitting alone at our kitchen table. It is an organic, *body* process. We need the feedback of the rest of the body to know what our bodily function is. This keeps us from thinking more highly of ourselves than we ought (Rom. 12:3). It also keeps us from deceiving ourselves into thinking we have one role in the body when other members of the body give us more accurate feedback to the contrary. We may not like it but it is generally more accurate than our self-evaluations.

I'm reminded of a twenty-something believer who kept presenting himself to others and me as someone with the gift of leadership. He certainly had the physical appearance of a leader (think Saul). The difficulty with his self-assessment was that no one was really following his "leading." Either this brother did not have the grace-gift of leadership or he thought too highly of himself (Rom. 12:3) and the Lord was withholding His blessings until the young leader could use his gifts with the motivation to edify others. The Bible presents the same solution to both problems: think of yourself with sound judgment by knowing who you are organically in the body of Christ (Rom. 12:3-8). If you have gifting in an area, the body will confirm it. Listen to the body of Christ's feedback and take it as Jesus' confirming or denying of your gifts.

5. Determine if your efforts are accompanied by God's blessing/fruit.

If a grace-gift is exercised in submission to the Spirit of God, blessing will accompany it. There will be spiritual success obvious to you and to others. What efforts in ministry is God blessing in your life? Which efforts seem to result in supernatural success each time?

One of the most wonderful things that members of the body of Christ do is mirror back gifting to one another. We should especially give feedback when we are blessed by the ministry of another's gifts. We should give a brother or sister in Christ immediate and encouraging feedback about how their use of a grace-gift blessed us. For example, it may be a person who:

- faithfully picks up extra paper and trash after a church service and we thank them for their service/helps
- quickly moves to express concern and grief to a body member who has received terrible news and we thank them for their mercy
- takes the time to pray boldly for us during a difficult time and we thank them for expressing their gift of faith
- has an encouraging word for us about a hard decision we face and we thank them for using their gift of exhortation or wisdom

Being attentive to God's people faithfully and fruitfully expressing their grace-gifts is immensely important for both the health of the body and the ongoing discovery of grace-gifts. This is true not just for speaking and leadership gifts, but especially for all of the less public gifts like serving/helps, mercy, giving, faith, distinguishing between spirits, etc. Local bodies of believers who are sensitized to recognizing and encouraging one another's gifts are on their way to becoming fully mobilized organisms whose saints are being equipped. They are the organic, sustainable church.

A BIT OF PERSPECTIVE

There are several wonderful ministries that I mentioned in Chapter Six that help Christians to discover their grace-gifts. Several of them take a very broad and holistic approach that includes attending to your personality and personal history. One of them uses the acronym S.H.A.P.E.: **S**piritual Gifts, **H**eart, **A**bilities, **P**ersonality, **E**xperiences.

I think that it is helpful to include all of these factors, however I would suggest that not all of them are equal in the process of discovering one's grace-gifts. I would suggest that the role of *Spiritual Gifts* is preeminent and the other four factors (Heart, Abilities, Personality, Experiences) should be secondary. This approach gives appropriate weight to the preeminent choices that a loving Heavenly Father has made for us: "But now God has placed the members, each one of them, in the body just as He desired" (1 Cor. 12:18). Essentially, our grace-gifts = our ministry role in the body of Christ, and this is God's choice. This gifting is the most important factor in discovering God's serving grace in our lives. The four other aspects either point to it, reflect it or correlate with it. But, they are not of equal importance.

A FAMILY NOTE

My wife Marty and I began teaching our children about grace-gifts when they were 10-12 years old. We also began to observe them and give them feedback about what their gifting might be as they entered their teenage years. We suggested that this information would be helpful to them in selecting their major field of study in college. This proved to be a very fruitful source of edification and encouragement to our family members, and it continues to this day. As my wife Marty and I continue to learn things about our roles in Christ's body, we continue to share our discoveries with our family. We also love to talk to our adult children and their mates about their roles.

In terms of Christian family members giving each other feedback about their respective grace-gifts, I was very impressed with a prayer letter we received last month from some dear Christian friends of almost thirty years, Tracy and Debra Weaver. In their letter they recounted how God gave them an unexpected gift as they gathered with their four children, plus two sons-in-law and grandmother, at Christmas. Here's what they wrote:

> When our whole family has the rare opportunity to be together, we like to be intentional about scheduling time for focused communication. With Sunday coming the day after Christmas, we chose to stay home for a special family time instead of attending church services. Debra had the idea of preparing a sheet with each of our family members' names across the top and a list of the spiritual gifts found in the Bible down the left side. (The term "spiritual gift" refers to the unique way the Holy Spirit expresses Himself through the life of each believer in Jesus Christ in order to build up the church—1 Cor. 12:7.)
>
> The plan was to focus on each family member and share with them the spiritual gifts that we observe operating in their life. There was no way we could have anticipated what was about to unfold. What was intended to be a brief session of light-hearted encouragement and affirmation became a deeply moving time of speaking into each other's heart and envisioning all that God may want to do in and through each family member. For three hours we used God's words, describing how He

expresses Himself through His children, as our vocabulary for describing the strengths, skills and abilities we see in each other's life. The time was filled with laughter and tears. It was unbelievably stirring.

As a father, I can't describe the joy of listening to our adult children speak words of blessing and life to one another. And then to have them share with Debra and me the spiritual gifts they see operating in our lives and how they have been a blessing to them and to others—*amazing!* No one was excluded. Grandma Barb (*G-mama*) and our sons-in-law, Brant and Evan, were all blessed and a blessing in all that was shared.

CONCLUSION

In this chapter I have suggested that there are five steps or aspects to the wonderful process of discovering the grace-gifts that Jesus the Messiah has given to each of us:

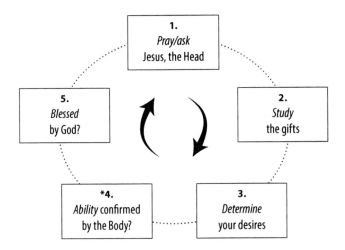

There is nothing mystical or magical about this process. It was simply derived by trying to think biblically and organically about how we discover the serving grace of God in our lives. Our prayer, knowledge about the gifts and desires for certain gifts/ministries are all important aspects of the process. Probably most important is the feedback from the body of Christ about what grace-gifts match up with the abilities that it has seen us display. One of our marvelous ministries in Christ's body is to mirror the reality of each other's grace gifting to each other. The body's feedback should take into account God's blessing (fruit) of our ministry efforts in its life. God's people know when they've been edified—blessed by God through us—and they are responsible to mirror that back to us as part of the organic life of Christ's body working to build itself up in love (Eph. 4:16).

Taking a grace-gifts test can also be very helpful in evaluating what ministries we desire to do and the ones that we think we do well in the body. Each of the five spiritual gifts books I mentioned in Chapter Six has a large section on grace-gifts, including a test the reader can take. I have also written a *Grace-Gifts Inventory* available for free at www.sustainablechurch.org. I encourage you to take an inventory and ask God's people who know you to confirm or modify your findings. Let the body of Christ speak to you about your role in the organic church. This will help sustain both you and the church in vibrant ministry that flows out of who you are in the body of Christ.

Chapter Ten

"BODY DISCIPLESHIP" CORRECTS "THE JESUS MODEL OF DISCIPLESHIP"

....

"After the Spirit comes, no discipleship takes place outside of the communities of faith and the goal of the communities themselves is to make people like Christ (Eph. 4:13). Perhaps the reason Jesus made provision for both the Spirit and for the church was the absolute necessity of both for accomplishing discipleship."

–James G. Samra[1]

Releasing and equipping the saints in the organic church is not an end in and of itself. It is a means to the end of "body discipleship." But before we can talk about that we must examine the dominant Western discipleship model that has hindered the expression of body discipleship for at least six decades. This dominant model has unknowingly contributed to the 1,900-year thwarting of the organic, sustainable church. So before we can build, we must blast a bit. Hopefully, out of the rubble a robust, biblical view of discipleship will emerge that beautifully expresses the organic church's sustainability.

THE IMPACT OF OUR CULTURAL GLASSES

I recently encountered a woman who had been in a Bible study I had taught over 15 years earlier. She vividly recounted an illustration that I had made when I wore bright yellow, comically over-sized sunglasses. I was trying to make the point that we all have glasses we have developed over the course of our lives. In the illustration I called them "worldviews," ways of seeing the world through culturally crafted lenses without even realizing that we have them. Among other things these cultural glasses shape our view of Christian discipleship.

For over 60 years the literature of the discipleship movement in the West has primarily originated with parachurch ministries. These groups have spawned discipleship philosophies and strategies appropriate to the Western individualistic "glasses" of the respective communities that shaped them:

- the American business community (Campus Crusade for Christ)

- the American military community (the Navigators)

- the American and United Kingdom academic communities (InterVarsity Christian Fellowship)

The result has been an individualistic emphasis in our discipleship methodologies that some have described as "the Jesus model of discipleship."[2]

I am a part of the fruit of all three of these wonderful parachurch ministries. Because of their shaping of my Christian life, I have struggled to reconcile my view of discipleship with the New Testament perspective. This chapter seeks to set forth a biblically informed view of discipleship that correlates with the organic gifting of the body of Christ and the equipping of the saints to do the work of ministry. To accomplish this goal we will need to drastically modify three of the main aspects of "the Jesus model of discipleship."

WHOSE DISCIPLES?

This illustration shows how "the Jesus model of discipleship" assumes that we should replicate what Jesus did with His 12 disciples with "our disciples":

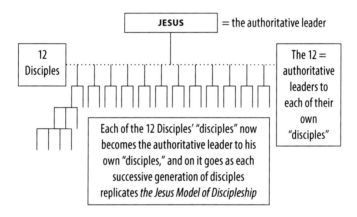

Calling fellow believers *our disciples* is closer to the discipleship model of Greek philosophy and rabbinical Judaism than to Jesus' model (Kittel, 431-41).[3] The Greek term for *disciple*, *mathētēs*, was used to refer to a member of a philosophical school, a student of medicine, or an apprentice of a trade in Hellenistic culture (Kittel, 438-40). In rabbinical Judaism a disciple attached himself to a teacher or rabbi in much the same manner as was done in Hellenistic culture. The disciple subordinated himself in almost servile fashion to his rabbi in order to learn all that the rabbi had to teach. In both the Hellenistic and Jewish cultures, the time spent as a disciple was only *transitory* until the disciple could become the teacher, rabbi, doctor, tradesman, etc. Also, the emphasis in both cultures was usually on *objective content* (e.g., learning a trade). There are notable exceptions like Socrates' methodology, but generally this observation holds true.

Ironically, the modern discipleship movement has adopted and used the Greek/rabbinical model even more rigidly than Jesus did. Even more ironically, we frame the Great Commission in terms of replicating this hierarchical approach in "the Jesus model of discipleship." What we have missed is how Jesus greatly modified the Greek/rabbinical discipleship model by emphasizing at least four unique aspects:

1. Being His disciple was not a transitory stage that one passed through on the way to a more sophisticated and respected level. Rather, being a disciple of Jesus was a *permanent relationship* and was the *climax* of every person's aspirations (Kittel, 448).

2. Jesus *called His disciples;* they did not select Him as their rabbi.

3. Jesus emphasized commitment to *His Person first*, and then commitment to objective content about His Person. In a sense these are inseparable, but according to Jesus' emphasis, the commitment to His Person, not just His teaching, was given priority (e.g., Mark 1:17, John 21:21-22).

4. Jesus emphasized *faith* in Him as the true test of His disciples' commitment (e.g., John 6:60-66). This emphasis is totally unique and unparalleled in Greek and Jewish culture.

It seems redundant to say that the making of disciples among the world's people-groups is the process of making disciples of *Jesus*, not us. We facilitate them becoming *His* disciples by teaching them to observe all that *He* commanded (Matt. 28:20). However, the widespread designation of Christians to whom we have ministered as "our disciples" necessitates underscoring this point. All Christians are disciples of Messiah Jesus, *not* of fellow believers. Dallas Willard beautifully captures this intention in Jesus' discipleship process:

> About two thousand years ago he gathered his little group of friends and trainees on the Galilean hillsides and sent them out to "teach all nations"—that is, *to make students (apprentices) to him from all ethnic groups.* His objective is eventually to bring all of human life on earth under the direction of *his wisdom, goodness, and power*, as part of God's eternal plan for the universe.[4]

An Application: Since every Christian is a disciple *of Jesus*, almost all of the 29 usages of *disciple* in Acts are used as synonyms for followers of Christ.[5] For example, in Acts 11:26c Luke says, "And in Antioch *the disciples* were first called Christians" (ESV). The New Testament usage also contradicts the widespread concept that *disciples* are especially committed Christians.[6] Instead, the key issue is, "*Now* that you *are* a disciple of Jesus, what *kind* of disciple are you going to be?" Moreover, as Christians we never "graduate" from being a disciple of Jesus and move on to being a disciple-maker (a rabbi). Rather, our ministry to others is always within the context of being Jesus' disciple.

WHY DIDN'T THE APOSTLES REPLICATE "THE JESUS MODEL OF DISCIPLESHIP"?

If the Great Commission was about the replicating of making individual disciples, then the twelve appear to have missed the assignment. However, as Acts and the epistles document, the apostles' understanding of the making of Jesus' disciples among the people-groups of the world caused them to focus primarily on the planting of *communities of believers—churches—*not on the discipling of individuals. With this approach, the apostles also faithfully maintained Jesus' central role as the discipler of all believers. Rather than functionally assuming Jesus' authoritative role, the apostles seemed to have followed this pattern of disciple-making:

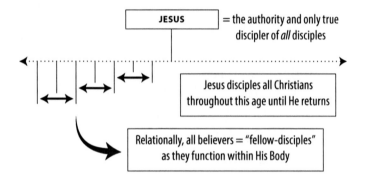

The apostles' view of disciple making does not replace Jesus with mature believers. Rather:

1. Christ Jesus is still "discipling" each believer in the strictest sense of the word. When we study the four Gospels and put ourselves in the disciples' place, we are learners who are becoming like our Teacher as we faithfully *follow Him* (e.g., Luke 6:40). Jesus' invitation to down-trodden sheep in Matthew 11:28-30 makes His ongoing discipling of each us abundantly clear:

   [28]*Come to Me*, all who are weary and heavy-laden, and *I will give you rest.* [29]*Take My yoke upon you, and learn from Me*, for *I am* gentle and humble in heart; and you will SHALL FIND REST FOR YOUR SOULS. [30]For *My yoke is easy, and My load is light.* (NASB; emphasis is mine)

Jesus also uses our involvement in the body of Christ to disciple us. We'll discuss that shortly.

2. Older, more mature believers still build into the lives of younger Christians, but not in a discipler/disciple sense *per se*. Rather, we should relate as *co-disciples* with each other as we all follow Christ as *His* disciples.

Note in Matthew 23:1-36 on Tuesday of passion week that Jesus vents His messianic spleen against the Pharisees for the final time. Particularly, in Matthew 23:8-12 He negates the entire hierarchical leadership structure of rabbinical Judaism:

> [8]But do not be called *Rabbi*; for One is your Teacher and you are all brothers. [9]And do not call anyone on earth *your father*; for One is your Father, He who is heaven. [10]And do not be called *mentors or spiritual guides;*[7] for One is your Mentor/Spiritual Guide, that is, Christ. [11]But the greatest among you shall be your servant. [12]And whoever exalts himself shall be humbled; and whoever humbles himself shall be exalted (my translation).

In these verses Jesus rejects all leadership relationships and titles among His people that create unnecessary spiritual hierarchies and *functionally* usurp His messianic role and that of God the Father. Instead, he opts for the servant-leader model that emphasizes brotherly relationships as fellow disciples. These verses have a very direct application to our contemporary views of disciple making. Particularly relevant is verse 8, where the focus is on claiming teaching authority (*rabbi-like*), and verse 10, which focuses on the leadership or guidance of a "master, mentor, spiritual guide or tutor" ("instructors" in ESV).[8]

Again, being a *disciple* of Christ is not a transitory role. The emphasis is upon working together as fellow-disciples to build into each other's lives as each one of us directly relates to Christ the discipler. Paul's use of peer terms to describe his "disciples" validates this as well. Paul *never* referred to any of the people he discipled (in the popular sense of the word) as "my disciple." In fact, the word *mathētēs, disciple, never occurs* in the Pauline epistles. Rather, Paul uses 17 different *sun*-cognates in Greek (*sun* meaning "with, co, or fellow" when combined with other nouns) to refer to those many would call "his disciples."[9]

1. "kinsman" (*suggenēs*) – Rom. 16:7, 11, 21 – of six different Christians

2. "fellow laborer" (*sunathleō*) – Phil. 4:3 – of Euodia and Syntyche (cf. Phil. 1:27)

3. "fellow prisoners" (*sunaichmalōtos*) – Rom. 16:7, Col. 4:10, Philem. 23

4. "fellow servants" (*sundoulos*) – Col. 1:7 (of Epaphras), 4:7 (of Tychicus)

5. "fellow traveler" (*sunekdēmos*) – 2 Cor. 8:19 – of Titus

6. "helpers/fellow workers" (*sunergos*) – Rom. 16:3, 9, 21 (of four Christians), 1 Cor. 3:9, 2 Cor. 1:24 (of the Corinthians), 8:23 (of Titus), Phil. 2:25 (of Epaphroditus), 4:3 (of Euodia and Syntyche), I Thess. 3:2 (of Timothy), Philem. 1 (of Philemon), v. 24 (of Demas and Lucas)

7. "fellow soldier" (*sustratiōtēs*) – Phil 2:25 (of Epaphroditus), Philem. 2 (of Archippus)

Paul also uses *ten* terms to refer to groups of Christians or to individuals in a less specific manner:

1. "be a fellow sufferer" (*sugkakopatheō*) – 2 Tim. 1:8 – to Timothy

2. "partakers/co-fellowshippers" (*sugkoinōnos*) – Phil 1:7 – of the Philippians

3. "yokefellow/comrade" (*suzugos*) – Phil. 4:3 – to the Philippians

4. "fellow partaker" (*summetochos*) – Eph. 3:6 – of the Gentiles

5. "fellow imitators" (*summimētēs*) – Phil. 3:17 – of the Philippians

6. "fellow citizens" (*sumpolitēs*) – Eph. 2:19 – of the Gentiles

7. "strive together with" (*sunagōnizomai*) – Rom. 15:30 – to the Romans

8. "co-helping" (*sunupourgeō*) – 2 Cor. 1:11 – of the Corinthians

9. "fellow body member" (*sussōmos*) – Eph. 3:6 – of the Gentiles

10. "fellow heir" (*sugklēronomos*) – Eph. 3:6 – of the Gentiles

An Application: I stopped calling others "my disciples" over 37 years ago when I studied more carefully the New Testament's teaching about discipleship. In the intervening years, I have continued to use peer terms like Paul did to refer to those I am privileged to serve. Additionally, *I relate as a fellow-disciple of Jesus*, not as "a discipler." This removes the pressure to try and *functionally* be Jesus to my fellow disciples. Only Jesus can be Jesus to His disciples. It is immensely important not to usurp Jesus'

unique authority by claiming a phantom discipleship authority
that the New Testament does not give us:

> Nowhere did Paul identify the role of "discipler" as a spiri-
> tual gift or as an office of the church. Rather, all Christians,
> both those imitating and those being imitated, are equal in
> the body of Christ. Paul's ability to hold these two in tension
> is a helpful example for spiritually mature leaders, who must
> acknowledge that they are on an equal footing with even the
> most immature Christian.[10]

Moreover, by relating as a fellow disciple of Jesus to those
around me, I can be free to continue to be "in process" as Jesus'
disciple and not only give, but also receive ministry from my
fellow believers. I have done this successfully with believers of
various levels of maturity, including new Christians and believers who were over 40 years younger than me. More mature
Christians opening themselves to mutual ministry in their relationships with younger believers also wonderfully models the
mutual ministry of the body of Christ and each member using
his or her gifts to build up the body. It expresses the inter-con-
nected heart of the sustainable church.

THE APOSTLES IMPLEMENTED "BODY DISCIPLESHIP"

The apostles primarily interpreted the discipleship charge of the
Great Commission in corporate, body of Christ terms, not in individualistic discipling terms. The primary means of both developing disciples in local churches and multiplying new communities
of believers (church-planting) is through "body discipleship."
Body discipleship is the body of Christ building itself up in
love *both qualitatively and quantitatively* through the proper
working of each individual body part equipped to discover and

use their spiritual gifts to fulfill the church's historical mission (Eph. 4:11-16).

"BODY DISCIPLESHIP"

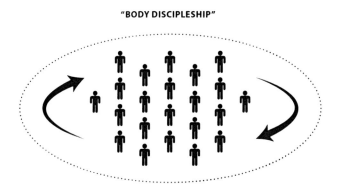

"…from whom the whole body, being fitted and held together by that which every joint supplies, according to the proper working of each individual part, causes the growth of the body for the building up of itself in love." (Ephesians 4:16 NASB)

The genius of body discipleship is that it connects the authority of Christ as the discipler of each believer with His role as the giver of grace-gifts to each believer (Eph. 4:7-10). Through both roles Jesus transforms His disciples and advances His mission of discipling all the people-groups of the world.

As has already been suggested, there is still a strategic need for working with individual believers à la 2 Timothy: "You therefore, my son, be strong in the grace that is in Christ Jesus. The things which you have heard from me in the presence of many witnesses, entrust these to faithful men who will be able to teach others also" (2 Tim. 2:1-2, NASB).

Ironically, within its biblical context, 2 Timothy 2:2 is actually a local church leadership development verse, not a basic discipleship verse. It is the elders of local churches who are specifically entrusted as "faithful men who will be able to teach others also."

This makes the qualification of being "able to teach others also" very specific to the leaders of local churches. The New Testament underscores that they are the ones responsible for overseeing and spearheading the teaching of Christians in local bodies. These are the ones that the New Testament synonymously calls "elders, shepherds and overseers" (e.g., Acts 20:17, 28 and 1 Peter 5:1-4). All three terms refer to the same leadership office in the New Testament. This is why the only "skill qualification" of the 20 qualifications for being an elder or overseer in 1 Timothy 3:1-7 and Titus 1:5-9 is "able to teach" (1 Tim. 3:2). More specifically, *an elder* (Titus 1:5)/*overseer* (Titus 1:7) should be characterized by "holding fast the faithful word which is in accordance with the teaching, that he may be able both to exhort in sound doctrine and to refute those who contradict" (Titus 1:9; NASB).

This leadership development should also be a robust emphasis of local churches. However, most would agree that the vast majority of the church's leaders in the West over the last 60 years has been developed primarily through parachurch ministries, not local churches. This is largely due to the institutional mindset of local churches and the institutions that train their vocational leaders. Since the end of World War II, parachurch ministries have stepped into this void and much of their "discipleship" has actually been *leadership development* for the body of Christ. Thank God for their ministries.

However, there are some significant blindsides to the leadership development of these parachurch ministries. My wife Marty and I realized this shortly after graduating from seminary when we met a young architect who had recently graduated from a wonderful school in Texas. He had been involved with one of the major parachurch ministries for all five years of his architectural program. However, it had been somewhat of a discouraging experience for him because he was never selected by the parachurch staff members to be in one of their small groups. Rather, he was always in a student-led small group. Their very clear message to him was that he did not know how to "move with the movers" and was not really a fruitful disciple-maker. The message conveyed was that he was not one of the "faithful men, who will be able to teach others also" (2 Tim. 2:2b). He wasn't on Jesus' varsity team. He was on the junior varsity.

As Marty and I got to know this young architect, we soon noticed that he had the grace gift of mercy. Given a thousand years, he would never have been a teacher of God's Word to others because that was not his role in the body of Christ. Instead, he was a very faithful and amazingly fruitful disciple of Jesus by being merciful to others. However, he had gotten caught in the inappropriate filter of the parachurch ministry. What they considered a "basic discipleship filter" was actually a "leadership filter." They were not so much doing basic discipleship with a 2 Timothy 2:2 emphasis, but rather they were doing leadership development. Unfortunately, they had unnecessarily discouraged many saints by creating too narrow of a filter for being a disciple of Jesus. Their filter probably caught many members of the body of Christ whose spiritual gifting did not correlate well with the parachurch ministry's emphasis.

The point of this story is that your process of growing as a disciple of Jesus should be synonymous with becoming aware of and developing the grace-gifts that Jesus has given to you. However, one of the downsides of any parachurch ministry is that it has narrowed the focus of grace-gifts to those that fulfill that particular ministry's purpose and advance its agenda. This is not wrong or sinful. It is just the nature of parachurch ministry. But this narrowing will winnow believers with divergent grace-gifts, confusing them and hindering their discovery of the role for which Jesus has gifted them.

This is why one's discipleship philosophy must be completely compatible with the New Testament's emphasis on grace-gifts, rather than working contrary to it. Unfortunately, replicating the hierarchical Jesus model of discipleship fails miserably at this compatibility. However, the more accurate view of Jesus discipling His people is that He directly teaches and mentors us through His Word and also directly disciples us through the use of our grace-gifts in community with others in the body of Christ. This is the genius of "body discipleship." It connects the authority of Christ as the discipler of each believer with His role as the Giver of spiritual gifts to each believer (Eph. 4:7-10). This is simply another beautiful expression of the organic, sustainable church.

CONCLUSION

The way out of the dual quagmires created by the overly individualistic orientation of the "Jesus model of discipleship" and the stifling institutional mindset of local churches is to emphasize afresh the "body discipleship" of the New Testament. However, to accomplish this we must first fit the leaders developed by parachurch ministries with "glasses" that value the organic, communal dimension of the church. *The church's leaders must be experts in nurturing communities that see, value, and mobilize the body of Christ by releasing and equipping the saints to do the work of ministry* (Eph. 4:11-13). They must see that the whole of the body's ministry is far greater than the sum of her individual parts. They must see that Jesus' discipling of His followers is integrally connected to His gifting of His followers. Equipping the saints and discipling the saints are two sides of the same coin. Both are crucial parts of the life of the organic church. Just like with His twelve apostles, Jesus disciples *us* to function in dynamic, organic community with one another. Any discipleship model that thwarts or undercuts that community is problematic. It may unwittingly underscore the hierarchical view of the pastor's role by introducing an unwarranted hierarchy of the "discipler" over the "disciple," which can prevent the releasing of *all the saints* to do the work of ministry in the organic, sustainable church.

Chapter Eleven

BODY DISCIPLESHIP IS THE HEART OF THE SUSTAINABLE CHURCH

....

"*Body discipleship* is the body of Christ building itself up in love *both qualitatively and quantitatively* through the proper working of each individual body part as the saints are equipped to discover and use their grace-gifts to fulfill the church's historical mission."

–Eph. 4:11-16

One of the many beauties of body discipleship is that it makes full use of all 19 grace-gifts distributed within Christ's body. Such an expression is exactly what is needed "to establish beachheads of Jesus' person, word, and power in the midst of a failing and futile humanity."[1] The diversity of the ministries represented by these gifts is almost limitless given the combinations of 2-3 gifts which most believers have. Therefore, opening one's self to Jesus working through the saints in a local body (and beyond) is opening one's self to vast spiritual resources which foster a holistic and in-depth discipleship process. Of course, this process is dependent upon the saints being nurtured and equipped so that they are fully functional and mobilized within the communal design of the body. This is why the discipleship process and the organic, sustainable church are so profoundly intertwined.

This contrasts with the limited grace gifting and ministry focus of *one person* who is your "discipler" in the Jesus model of discipleship. Though unintentionally, this popular Western discipleship approach essentially ignores the vast communal resources of God's people. Such an individualistic approach to discipleship also fits rather nicely with our view of personal identity in the Western part of the world. The "Western Narcissistic Self" described below has been crafted over the last several hundred years in the West.[2] The most troublesome aspect of it for our purposes is that it clashes quite directly with a vibrant participation in the sustainable church:

THE CONTRAST OF

THE WESTERN NARCISSISTIC SELF	BIBLICAL SELF-IDENTITY
1. an individual thing, self-sufficient and self-contained	1. deeply embedded in our social identity of being in Messiah's and God's family
2. with sharply-defined personal boundaries	2. such that our individual boundaries are relatively undefined due to connection to Christ and His people
3. that hide the real me in my "inner depths"	3. so that our real self is communicated through the fruit of our behavior
4. as I depend upon my capacity for autonomous and self-generated action.	4. as we achieve "authentic" living through obedience to and dependence upon others.

My concern is that the overly individualistic approach to discipleship may unwittingly reinforce some of the unbiblical, unhealthy aspects of our radical Western individualism. Let me again say that I whole-heartedly support the role of *one-on-one encouragement of fellow disciples by every Christian* and also *the one-on-one leadership development with certain believers.* I have done this several hours every week for over 45 years and I delight in it. However, it is certainly no substitute for a believer being discipled by Jesus Christ through *many* of the grace-gifted members of His body.

THE SPECTRUM OF RELATIONAL CLOSENESS

When we speak of Jesus discipling His followers through the ministry of the body of Christ, we must recognize that there will be a wide range in the relational closeness of those who Jesus uses to minister to us. Let me try and picture this relational spectrum:

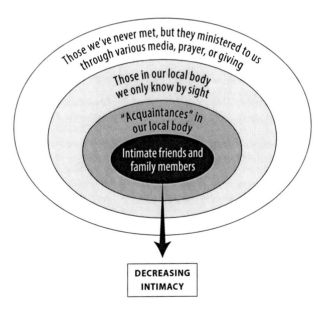

The point of this diagram is that God will likely use thousands of fellow saints over the course of our lives to grow us as disciples of Jesus. Some will be very close to us; some will be absolute strangers. Some will minister to us in major ways and most will minister to us in minor ways. The point is that all of these disciples of Jesus will contribute to our personal discipleship by Jesus. The almost unlimited variety of the expression of their grace-gifts will have a cumulative, transforming effect on us over the course of our life in Christ. This is the beauty of "body discipleship."

WHAT DOES BODY DISCIPLESHIP LOOK LIKE?

How does body discipleship occur within this relational spectrum? Let's revisit *Last Evangelical Organic Church* from Chapter Three. It is a church of 200 members, all equipped to know, develop and exercise their grace-gifts. While they are at different stages of spiritual maturity, every member is delightfully functional within the body. Let's look at two different individuals and how Jesus used them in body discipleship within this sustainable church. Though the names are changed, these two accounts of saints' lives actually happened. I witnessed them first-hand over several years and both played a meaningful role in my discipleship by Jesus.

A MIDDLE-AGED RECOVERING ALCOHOLIC

George had grown up in a home with an alcoholic father. One of George's vivid family memories was that he and his dad were in the drunk-tank together in their Southern California hometown. George had started drinking at an early age and had about 30 years of alcohol damage in his body by the time he was in his mid-40s. Thankfully George chose to place his faith in Christ around this time and began to move into sobriety, attempting to repair his relationship with his wife and three children. I met George when he was still early in this process and still pretty immature spiritually, due to the lack of teaching in his previous church.

When George and his wife became a part of our church—we called it "joining the ministry team"—all of these tender issues in their lives were shared very openly and honestly. While there was lots of hurt and damage, there was the grace of God and the healing of the Holy Spirit at work in their lives. Nevertheless, George was ready for me when I sat down to talk to him about "his ministry" in the church. Such a thought was so far-fetched to him that he uncharacteristically went on the offensive with me. Before I could even ask him about his desires and gifting for ministry, George preempted me: "I don't read too good; I don't write too good; and I certainly don't talk too good!"

His assessment of himself was that he was absolutely worthless in ministry and there was no use in trying to convince him otherwise. I had known men like George in the churches of my youth and they tended to lurk on the fringes of the fellowship, just trying to blend into the woodwork. They would get lost in the vast majority of churches because they weren't readers, writers, and talkers. However, we were profoundly committed to releasing all of the saints in our young church by helping them discover and put to use their grace-gifts in our ministry together. So, by faith, I looked him in the eye and said with a smile on my face, "George, I'm not buying your package! We're going to keep at it until we figure out how Jesus has gifted you and how He wants you to minister." I realized by what George said to me about his reading, writing and speaking that he had a very narrow, pastor-centric view of ministry. It was going to be a challenge to widen George's horizons about the Spirit's amazing grace-gifts.

Well, it didn't take long to figure out that George had the gifts of *helping and serving*. Additionally, it came out that he loved to work on machines and had amazing mechanical aptitude. Considering my vast incompetence in that area, I was quickly in profound admiration of his abilities and I told him so. I could see that my respect for him in this area gave him a bit of confidence and bolstered his faith that there might be some type of ministry where he could lead from his strengths and not from his weaknesses. So, with George's permission we announced to our church that George had natural abilities with mechanical things and that he enjoyed helping and serving others as a part of "his ministry." I was one of the first to ask him to help me fix a dishwasher in our home that stopped working. George quickly and easily fixed it and I immediately became his press agent.

Fast-forward 25 years to when I visited George in this same church, which Marty and I had helped plant a quarter of a century earlier. I had left the church several years earlier and was now a stuffy seminary professor. But when I saw George, I couldn't help asking him to tell me about "his ministry." Though he was immensely humble, he beamed from ear-to-ear as he shared about how God had used him in his ministry. I asked him how many people he had probably helped over the years, but he hadn't kept count. I said, "George, is it probably hundreds and hundreds of folks?" But he wouldn't be specific. So I countered with, "Is it thousands of others that you have ministered to, George?" But again, he didn't want to brag. However, he did say with tears in his eyes that he had such unspeakable delight in being able to use his grace-gifts to serve Christ in this manner.

Here is the takeaway from George's amazing ministry. He had a quarter-of-a-century of fruitfulness for Christ because a young, obstinate pastor wanted him to join in the fun. Again, someone like George would be caught in the filter of 99.9% of churches because he didn't have the typical skills, education or persona that we associate with "ministry." But shame on us for being so limited in our view of the grace-gifts that the Spirit has given and in the innumerable applications that those gifts can have in the body of Christ and beyond. I know that George's ministry to me had positively impacted my relationship with Christ just like it had countless others. Not a great reader, writer or speaker, but a very faithful, grace-gifted saint who had an astonishing ministry for Christ by simply being who God had made him to be and not trying to be someone or something he was not.

My question for you is: "How many Georges have we overlooked in our churches who could have had ministries for decades if we had eyes to see how they could contribute to body discipleship?" Both we and they are the poorer spiritually because of our truncated view of what "ministry" is. How impoverished we are because we conceive of ministry as focusing on and centering around the gifts of one or two shepherds rather than arrayed around the dizzying diversity of the grace-gifted sheep. God forgive us.

A REPENTANT, BROKEN WOMAN

There is a woman named Dorothy at Last Organic who had a hard life well into middle age because she was married to an alcoholic. Because of her husband's passive-aggressive personality and lack of leadership in the home, Dorothy hungered for meaningful emotional connection with a man. A few years before I met her, Dorothy had had a brief affair with a pastor who was counseling her. However, Dorothy had confessed it to her church, repented of her actions and had submitted to her church's discipline. Dorothy was an honest and courageous woman who wanted to grow in Christ and walk faithfully with

Him in the midst of her trying circumstances. Nevertheless, in the eyes of many churches, Dorothy would have carried the stigma of being "a fallen woman," vastly limiting her ministry opportunities. Thankfully, that was not the case at Last Organic. Dorothy's past sin was not held against her due to her confession, repentance and restoration. Most people in the church only knew Dorothy as a tenderhearted, growing believer in Christ who was gifted as an empathetic listener and wise counselor.

When she reached her 40s, Dorothy began to have a remarkable counseling ministry in the church, due in part to encouragement of us elders to help equip Dorothy to use her gifts of exhortation and wisdom. Someone suggested that she seek advice and mentoring from a local Christian counselor who had her doctorate in psychology. Additionally, our church sent Dorothy to several Christian counseling conferences and bought the sets of videos of those training conferences for her. Dorothy learned from these training videos and also recruited many others in the body who had similar gifting and interests to share in the video training courses. This led to the development of our church's counseling ministry, which helped innumerable saints work through their problems in a godly manner.

Along the way, the elders asked Dorothy to spend time with those in the church who were preparing to be sent out in teams as cross-cultural missionaries. It is widely documented that many of the problems that occur on the mission field are due to the missionaries not being able to get along with their teammates. We decided to try to equip our missionary teams with relational and communication skills so that they would be as prepared as possible for the relational rigors in their cross-cultural settings. Dorothy was the obvious leader of this training. Over the years she had an astonishing impact on about thirty or more missionary candidates, many of whom she visited and ministered to while they were on the mission field.

The last time I visited this church I was invited to meet with the elders. I discovered that Dorothy had also been invited to sit in on their elder meetings *every week*. They realized that they needed her wisdom and exhortation to help them relate to one another in a more meaningful and godly manner during their meetings. As I observed her, Dorothy was her typical wise and skillful self in helping to equip these men to relate in a manner that was pleasing to Christ.

It was during this visit that I got to spend a little bit of time with Dorothy. I didn't realize that it would be the last time I would see her smiling face this side of eternity. During our conversation I asked, "Dorothy, tell me about your ministry?" Dorothy told me she was leading a group of young men in their 20s and 30s who had been sexually assaulted earlier in their lives. I was astonished. "Dorothy, these are really very complex and heavy issues! How is it going?" She told me that she was still working under the tutelage of the Christian psychologist and that the group was going amazingly well. I'm sure that these wounded younger brothers in Christ were greatly encouraged by this mature, godly woman who understood and identified with their emotional pain and suffering. Over the years Dorothy had learned how to trust Christ each day and let Him heal the depths of her pain as only He can. There was great healing and great wisdom in her words to these young men.

I hope you can appreciate the unspeakable beauty of Dorothy's ministry. May I again remind you that this was a saint with minimal formal education (high school). However, she was an immensely hungry *lifelong learner* and was motivated to use her grace-gifts maximally. In the end she had *an international ministry* through her on-going training of over thirty missionaries, an astonishing counseling ministry using her gifts of exhortation and wisdom to help hundreds of saints in the United States, and an incredibly rich impact on Last Organic Church through the weekly wisdom and encouragement that she gave its elders.

How many Dorothys do we have in our non-organic churches who have not been led to repentance and through a restoration process? How many Dorothys do we have sitting in the penalty box after restoration? How many Dorothys have we overlooked because these saints did not have college degrees? Do we assume that these degrees are absolutely necessary for a meaningful ministry for Christ? (Note that the person asking this question has spent the last 25 years as a professor in undergraduate and graduate education.) Jesus' twelve disciples likely had a 3rd or 4th grade elementary education.[3] However, like Dorothy, they were vibrant life-long learners in Christ, as evidenced by their writings in the New Testament (1-2 Peter, The Gospel of John, 1, 2, 3 John and Revelation). Once disciples of Jesus discover their grace gifting, their motivation to learn and serve Him is dynamically fueled by both *their intrinsic motivation* and by the Holy Spirit. They want to be who Jesus has gifted them to be. The boundaries of the resulting ministries are astonishing indeed.

BODY DISCIPLESHIP AND THE SUSTAINABLE CHURCH

These are only two of numerous examples of ordinary saints who had 25-30 years of rich, vibrant ministry and a profound impact on the spiritual growth of countless others in Christ. I can personally testify that Jesus used both Dorothy and George (and hundreds of others) in Last Organic Church to build into my life as His disciple. I regularly think of both of them and draw great encouragement from their faithfulness and from the phenomenal design of the body of Christ. If only we could see the power and beauty of the organic, sustainable church in the midst of the organizational complexities of the non-organic church.

Rather than being centered on the gifts and ministries of *a handful of "professionals,"* the sustainable church is fueled by the ministries of those who mobilize, equip, and release *all the saints* to enter into the joy of the ministry *given to the whole body of Christ.* We will all be spiritually richer because of this saints-centered ministry. Why? *Because body discipleship is the heart that fosters the organic life of the sustainable church.*

The discipleship of Jesus followers was never meant to be a process so totally dependent on a small percentage of Christians who are paid to help the saints grow. While these leaders can and should have a significant impact, they are not the engine that sustains discipleship. *Jesus* is the engine. He primarily does this in and through the healthy, organic functioning of those He has gifted to contribute to the discipleship process. Who is that? All believers in Messiah Jesus who He has gifted to share in the work of ministry/service. Such a broadly and richly gifted body of believers is an organism designed to reproduce itself continually and sustain itself perpetually until Messiah Jesus returns. This ongoing manifestation of Jesus' serving grace is the organic, sustainable church. May God help us to discover the richness of this aspect of His manifold grace.

Chapter Twelve

"MOSES MODEL LEADERS"
NEED NOT APPLY

....

What is a "Moses model leader"? It is a term that has been used for many years in church growth circles to describe a vision-casting leader. The assumption is that as Moses led Israel out of Egypt, so will a Moses model leader lead *his church* into "the promised land." The assumption is that churches need to a strong, visionary leader with the skills to implement his vision for his local church. This pastor needs to be the one person that both church members and seekers identify as the leader of this particular local church. As we will discuss in this chapter, this view of leadership usurps Jesus' role as the head of His church.

I once consulted with a church that was transitioning to a multiple leadership model—a shared-teaching model. When some older congregants heard about the transition, they posed a very pointed question to the elders and I in a congregational meeting: "If we have shared teaching, whose name are we going to put on the church sign as the head pastor?" I quickly responded with, "Why don't you put *Jesus' name* on the sign as the Chief Shepherd of this church." They were not the least bit happy with me. It was as if a church without a single pastor's name on its sign was a church without an identity. How did we get here?

A growing, thriving church that my wife and I helped to start grew from six couples to about 900 people in its first seven years. During this time we had also helped plant three other churches with various groups from our congregation and were in the process of training 20-25 folks to be sent out as missionaries to unreached people groups. Among the distinctions of this church—in addition to an every-member-ministry—was the idea that Jesus was the head. This meant that our under-shepherds (elders) existed to implement Chief Shepherd Jesus' will for our local body. We discerned His will by discussing and praying until we were of one heart and mind.

However, when one of our under-shepherds went to a church growth conference, he came back persuaded *that churches grow large faster when they have one shepherd other than Jesus with whom people can identify.* Before his "conversion," he had told the conference experts that we had grown large in the 5-6 years of our existence by implicitly pointing people to identify with Jesus as the head pastor. This was the growth experts' response: "Your church is an aberration, a fluke, and it should not have grown! You cannot grow a church without a focus on just one communicator with whom seekers can identify."

Somehow in developing our theology of leadership, we must have missed the memo that church growth demands a single preaching pastor as the focal point. Instead, we were committed to fostering *His* sustainable church with a focus on every-member ministry and reproducing other local bodies of believers. Why, we even committed another unpardonable sin in the eyes of these church growth experts by choosing to rent space in a school rather than own property in the community. We were criticized for trying to be good stewards of the money God's people gave by minimizing facilities costs and investing in people rather than brick-and-mortar.

Some of our dear friends were a part of a church plant by an evangelical church and its denomination. This young church plant had amazing body life and a marvelous every-member ministry for its first few years, while not having a vocational pastor. The plot thickened a bit when the denomination appointed a person to be the church's shepherd. When problems eventually arose with this shepherd that couldn't be resolved internally, the congregation appealed to his denominational superior. Within a short time, the superior dissolved and dismissed the local congregation and backed the shepherd. He made it very clear by his actions that the sheep were replaceable, but apparently *the shepherds were not.*

Our friends were bemoaning the loss of their local body to us a short time later. In light of major theological concerns about this denomination that I had been raising with them for some time, this was my sensitive, caring response:

> Wow! I guess theology really does matter. When the chips were down, this denomination's leadership theology became very evident. Theologically, they don't see the sheep, but the ordained shepherd as *the defining element of the church.* The church goes on because the shepherd is there, even if the sheep are not!

How did we get here?

OUR THEOLOGY OF LEADERSHIP REALLY DOES MATTER

The examples I shared really did happen and they are from three different denominations. This is not unusual because our defective theology of leadership is widespread, spanning the denominational spectrum. How did we arrive at a leadership theology where the identity of a church, the growth of a church and even the definition of the church all center in the singular ordained leader and not in the saints? How could we derive a theology of leadership with such pride and privilege when we start with a leader like *Moses?*

> Now the man Moses was very humble, more than any man who was on the face of the earth. (Num. 12:3)

And how can we perpetuate this leader-centric focus when we culminate in *Messiah Jesus,* the Leader of leaders?

> ⁶who, although He existed in the form of God, did not regard equality with God a thing to be grasped, ⁷but emptied Himself, taking the form of a bond-servant, and being made in the likeness of men. ⁸Being found in appearance as a man, He humbled Himself by becoming obedient to the point of death, even death on a cross. (Phil. 2:6-8)

How did we get here?

The short answer is that we got here the same way we got to our defective theology of the saints' ministry. We commingled ideas about leadership from popular culture with the Bible's theology of leadership. We then called it *tradition.* As *tradition* it soon became sacred, normative, widely accepted. Along the way we started calling it "Christian." Of course, the acid test was and always is, "How does such a theology stand up to the Bible's clear teaching?" Let's pour out that biblical acid and find out.[1]

First, our theology of leadership in the non-organic church is largely functionally defined and skills-centric. It is a modernity-fueled reduction from the lofty view of leadership found in the Bible. For example, the New Testament emphasizes the development of virtues as the primary qualifiers for leadership in an elder's/pastor's character. 19 of the 20 elder qualities in 1 Timothy 3 and Titus 1 focus on these virtues. Only one quality focuses on a skill: *able to teach.* According to the Bible, 95% of the emphasis in determining who should lead should focus on character. The remaining 5% of emphasis should be on the one skill of teaching the flock the Word of God. However, in our culture we regularly emphasize *skills and gifts* over *character*. The majority of the time, God's people will readily substitute gifts for character when looking for a leader. "Leadership development" gets viewed as skills acquisition with minimal emphasis on character development. This has contributed to our shrunken theology of leadership in the church and to an unbiblical focus and paradigm: skills over character.

Secondly, as I already noted, one of the core tenets for growing a church over the last generation is that a church must have a single pastor or a senior pastor who spearheads the vision of the church and with whom seekers can identify. It has been observed that the world's twenty largest churches manifest this pattern,[2] "the Moses model of leadership." As Moses envisioned and led Israel to the Promised Land, so should the senior pastor cast the vision and lead his church to growth. Such a dynamic view of leadership has been alluring to many frustrated and defeated pastors. On the one hand, I applaud the ministry of encouragement this has been to them. Pastoral ministry is extremely difficult in North America in light of the unrealistic expectations for personal fulfillment that most people have.[3] On the other hand, this leadership model is defective theologically and has led to the impotence of the non-organic church.

THE NEW TESTAMENT'S "NEW MOSES"

Theologically, the Old Testament anticipates and the New Testament authenticates that there will be "the new Moses leadership model." Moses himself exhorts Israel in Deuteronomy 18:15 to expect a prophet like him who will come in Israel's future to whom they must listen: "The Lord your God will raise up for you a prophet like me from among you, from your countrymen, you shall listen to him." The New Testament makes it clear that Messiah Jesus is that prophet, the new Moses. There is a consistent emphasis in John's Gospel (and somewhat in Acts) that Jesus is the second or new Moses who is far greater than the first. For example, while the Torah was given through Moses, Jesus himself is the New Torah because He has seen the Father and explains him (John 1:17-18). While manna was given through Moses, Jesus himself is the true manna from heaven (John 6:32-35). Because Jesus supersedes Moses, ascriptions such as "life," "light," "bread" and "water," previously used of the Mosaic Torah, are now applied to Jesus.[4]

Perhaps the most vivid example of Jesus as the new Moses is in John 6:1-13, where Jesus performs the messianic miracle of feeding the 5,000 in the wilderness. When He finishes feeding the multitude, He still has twelve baskets of barley loaf fragments left over. Notice the response of the people:

> Therefore when the people saw the sign which He had performed, they said, "*This is truly the Prophet who is to come into the world*." So Jesus perceiving that they were intending to come and take Him by force to make Him king, withdrew again to the mountain by Himself alone (John 6:14-15; my emphasis).

It is clear that the Moses model of leadership is, in fact, a New Testament phenomenon. *But it is a leadership model that is only to be filled by Messiah Jesus and Him alone*. To speak of the Moses model of leadership and apply it to a pastor or to any Christian leader is to usurp the role of the *true* New Testament Moses. This is a significant theological misunderstanding and a fallacious foundation for a popular church leadership model. Of course, you can set yourself forth as the Moses-type leader of a local church if you want it to be a non-organic church centered on you and not on our organic church leader, Messiah Jesus. Of course, the quality and sustainability of your attempt at Moses-like leadership compared to the new Moses will eventually be evident to all (compare Heb. 3:1-6).

JESUS AS THE CHIEF SHEPHERD/SENIOR PASTOR

In addition to usurping Jesus' role as the new Moses, we have misunderstood how He expresses His role as the Chief (senior) Shepherd in relation to a local church. This is a remarkable claim. Fortunately, six passages in the Old and New Testaments validate this claim. Ezekiel 34 is a remarkable chapter within the exilic prophet Ezekiel's prophecies about Israel's past and future. Ezekiel, a prophetic contemporary of Jeremiah, experienced the destruction of Judah and the exile during his lifetime. While in Babylon, he recorded the Lord God's *woe oracle* in Ezekiel 34:1-10 where God fires the shepherds of Israel. The term "shepherds" normally included not only Israel's political shepherds (kings), but also the spiritual shepherds (the priests and prophets).[5] God removed them from tending His flock Israel because they neglected the needs of the flock in order to care for their own needs. They exploited God's people and let them be destroyed while profiting off of them (see also Jer. 23:1-8).

However, Ezekiel also brings *a blessing oracle* for God's flock in this chapter: "Yahweh Himself will shepherd His people" (Ezek. 34:11-24). The Lord God will search for and rescue His sheep *by His own hand*. He will do this by placing over them His designated ruler:

> [23]Then I will set over them *one shepherd, My servant David*, and he will feed them; he will feed them himself and be their shepherd. [24]And I, the Lord, will be their God, and My servant David will be prince among them; I the Lord have spoken. (Ezek. 34:23-24; my emphasis)

Under Yahweh's servant David, He will restore His flock to their land and rescue them from their plight by making "a covenant of peace" with them (v. 25; cf. Ezek. 37:24), gathering them from the nations and blessing their land (vv. 25-31). Therefore, in Ezekiel 34, the Lord God establishes His future pattern for the shepherding of His people.

From the New Testament perspective, it is quite obvious that Jesus of Nazareth is the greater David appointed by the Father to shepherd His people. We see this in four New Testament passages. In Matthew 9:35-38, Jesus expresses the care of a true shepherd by going about the cities and villages and teaching, proclaiming the gospel of God and healing every disease and sickness (v. 35). He also expresses the concern of Yahweh's shepherd as He observes the shepherdless flock:

> [36]Seeing the people, He felt compassion for them, because they were distressed and dispirited like sheep without a shepherd. [37]Then He said to His disciples, "The harvest is plentiful, but the workers are few. [38]Therefore, beseech the Lord of the harvest to send out workers into His harvest." (Matt. 9:36-38)[6]

In John 10:1-18, Jesus is more overt and claims that He is "the door of the sheep" and the only way of deliverance for them (vv. 7-10). Even more vividly, He claims, "I am the good shepherd; the good shepherd lays down His life for the sheep" (v. 11). In contrast to a hireling who flees when the wolf comes (vv. 12-13), Jesus will not flee because of His concern for the flock (v. 13b). As the good shepherd, He knows His own and lays down His life for them (vv. 14-15). He is the one designated by the Father to unify God's flock:

> [16]I have *other sheep*, which are not of this fold; I must bring them also, and they will hear My voice; and they will become *one flock with one shepherd.* [17]For this reason the Father loves Me, because I lay down My life so that I may take it again. [18]No one has taken it away from Me, but I lay it down on My own

initiative. I have *authority* to lay it down, and I have *authority* to take it up again. *This commandment* I received from My Father. (John 10:16-18; my emphasis)

I suggest to you that Jesus' claim to be the good shepherd is the claim to be the Davidic Messianic Servant whom the Father has designated—fully authorized—to shepherd God's people. This includes not only God's historic people Israel, but also the "other sheep which are not of this fold" which are to become "one flock with one shepherd" (John 10:16).[7] John 10:1-18 completes the theological loop begun in Ezekiel 34. In fact, we cannot fully understand John 10 unless we understand Ezekiel 34. God's shepherding of His people is fully delegated to the God-man, Messiah Jesus. He is the *only one authorized* to die for the flock and to rise again for the flock. What a God! What a Shepherd!

Two New Testament passages take the historical fact of Jesus' role as the designated shepherd of God's people and apply it in a pastoral manner to two groups of people within local churches. In 1 Peter 2:25 the apostle applies Jesus' shepherding of our souls to those servants who are suffering unjustly at the hands of their masters: "For you were continually straying like sheep, but now you have returned to the Shepherd (*poimēn*) and Guardian (*episkopos*) of your souls." In 1 Peter 5:4, Peter concludes his encouragement of the elders/pastors of local churches who are to shepherd the flock of God voluntarily, eagerly and as examples (vv. 1-3). If you local church under-shepherds pastor in this manner, "when the Chief Shepherd (*archipoimēn*) appears, you will receive the unfading crown of glory."

Perhaps we can now understand why the title *leaders* is never used by Paul to refer to those who shepherd Jesus' flock:

It is all the more significant when we come to Paul's view of leadership in the context of the church, therefore, to note that he avoids the terms "leader" or "leadership" with reference to Christian communities, preferring to speak rather of service or ministry (διακονία) and co-workers.[8]

Apparently, certain titles cross the line and usurp Jesus' role as our leader and "senior pastor." As the new Moses who leads us, Messiah Jesus is:

- the Chief Shepherd (1 Pet. 5:4)

- the Good Shepherd (John 10:11, 14)

- the Great Shepherd of the sheep (Heb. 13:20)

- the Shepherd and Guardian of your souls (1 Pet. 2:25)

God forbid that we would theologically, or even functionally, usurp His unique role as our singular *shepherd and leader*. How does this fit with *your* church's "leadership" functions, roles and titles?

IS JESUS THE SENIOR PASTOR OF EACH LOCAL CHURCH?

If Yahweh committed to replace His people's shepherds with His own shepherd—the Davidic Messiah Jesus—then why would He then turn around and give the primary shepherding of His people back to other shepherds? Why would God intend for this messianic shepherding to be so vague and ethereal in concept that it had no meaningful local expression of shepherding by the Greater David? How does this accomplish God's purpose of providing the sacrificial and exacting care for His people that Israel's shepherds did not accomplish?

I have sought to validate in this chain of biblical passages that Jesus the Messiah is the shepherd of God's whole (universal) flock. But does Jesus' role as chief shepherd also apply to each local expression of the universal flock? Is it theologically likely that the risen, ruling Messiah Jesus is truly the chief shepherd–the chief or senior pastor–of each local flock? I believe that this is theologically inescapable from the Bible's teaching about Jesus. But I also believe that it has been covered over by our mystical, ahistorical view of the risen Christ's present ministry. What the Old and New Testaments proclaimed as Jesus' very specific shepherding ministry in space-time history, we have turned into "mystical mush."

Mystical mush does not walk among local churches like the Chief Shepherd does (Rev. 2:1). As He walks among His local churches, Jesus also:

- personally removes lampstands [churches] (Rev. 2:5)

- makes war against them with the sword of His mouth (Rev. 2:16)

- makes sick and kills those who lead believers astray (Rev. 2:20-23)

- comes like a thief in the night to a sleeping church (Rev. 3:3)

- humbles the synagogue of Satan (Rev. 3:9)

- stands outside the door of the house where a wealthy, lukewarm church meets and knocks to come in to have fellowship with those who hear the Chief Shepherd's voice (Rev. 3:20)

This certainly appears to me to be pretty hands-on involvement in the life of each of the seven churches of Asia in Revelation 2-3. Is Jesus' shepherding of these local churches normative for all local churches? I certainly think so.

However, we can hardly recognize the reigning, ruling Messiah's role in our theology of local church "leadership" because we are functionally so pragmatic and theologically so mystical. With our hollow view of Messiah Jesus' shepherding of the church, we easily move to fill the vacuum with our own conceptions of leadership. We end up with senior pastors and pastors of every type and title who *functionally* fulfill the role that God has only delegated to Messiah Jesus. We usurp our habitation as *under-shepherds* and encroach upon the God-Man's authority as *over-shepherd.*

By inappropriately elevating the role of under-shepherds with titles like "senior pastor" or "the Moses model of leadership," we ironically devalue them. We stake our claims on turf that belongs solely to Jesus and thereby diminish the terrain that we *are* supposed to inhabit. We must be immensely careful not to glorify alleged qualities of leadership that may many times be simply pragmatic or even fleshly strategies contrived to glorify ourselves. In the process we may miss the qualities that should characterize godly under-shepherds and true leaders of God's flock: a humble, tender heart that hears the Chief Shepherd's voice and carries out *His will.* We have a defective theology of leadership that all too often results in the flock looking for something from their under-shepherds that only the Chief Shepherd could give them.

Does this mean that there is no room for visionary shepherding in the church? Not at all. In fact, a significant leadership crisis has been emerging for some time in evangelicalism. However, what the biblical passages we discussed establish is *the nature of leading* in the church. Jesus explicitly says that we are *not* to lead in the church like the Gentiles (pagans) lead in the broader culture (Matt. 20:20-28/Mark 10:35-45). Strong, visionary Christian shepherding is to be under our true leader, Messiah Jesus, and is to be *humble and servant-like* to the body of Christ like Jesus' servant-leadership (Matt. 20:26-28/Mark 10:43-45). We are servant-leaders from *among, not over* God's people in a hierarchical sense (e.g., Acts 20:28; 1 Pet 5:1a). While the flock submits to our delegated authority to keep watch over their souls, we who are leaders should be ever mindful that we do so "as those who will give an account" (Heb. 13:17c).

CONCLUSION

What does all this mean for the sustainable, organic church and her equipping of the saints? It means *we should "lead" in light of Jesus' vision for our local body as reflected in His gifting of the members and in the collective heart and passion for ministry His flock possesses.*

I cannot emphasize this point enough. The under-shepherds' vision for ministry for a local church is therefore informed by the personality of the flock and tempered by the resources that Jesus has graciously given to that local congregation. *Both the authority to shepherd and the resulting vision for ministry are derived from the Good Shepherd.* Our task as under-shepherds is to determine what emphasis in ministry *Jesus* has given us through the grace-gifts of our local body. The vision for a local church is *an organic thing* coming from each church's collective giftedness. Therefore, we use our delegated authority as delegated under-shepherds who function as delegated servant-leaders who are supposed to equip God's people to fulfill the delegated vision. What do we have that does not flow from Jesus' hand? It is all derived from and delegated by Him.

This is why our titles should match our delegated, under-shepherd roles. Perhaps this diagram will help to contrast the key elements of the so-called "Moses model of leadership" and what I think is the New Testament's model of leadership:

THE CHURCH

| WITH A "MOSES MODEL" LEADER | WITH JESUS AS THE SENIOR PASTOR |

1. **Starting Point:** The Moses model leader. The vision/emphasis comes from this Moses-type leader in light of his gifts and interests and successful models. He then imprints his vision upon the local body. New senior pastor = new church vision/ emphasis.

2. **Role of the Leaders:** To embrace and communicate the senior pastor's vision for ministry, to implement that vision/emphasis throughout the church, and to equip the saints to do the work of ministry associated with fulfilling that vision.

3. **The Unity of the Church:** It is largely extrinsic and functional in that it is built around embracing the latest leadership emphasis & successful model.

4. **Continuity in the Church's Ministry:** It is contingent upon the attracting/repelling response to the senior pastor and his vision/emphasis for this local church. A change in the Moses model leader many times causes a radical shift in the philosophy of ministry that reshuffles the saints. Older saints hunker down and stay; younger ones leave and find a new leader they like more.

1. **Starting Point:** Jesus and His gifts. Jesus, the Chief Shepherd/Senior Pastor, has gifted each local church with a specific ministry through the collective grace-gifts of the body. Growth enriches but doesn't radically change the collective gifting.

2. **Role of the Under-Shepherds:** To point all to Jesus, the true senior pastor, to determine His will for this local body by discerning its collective gifting, and to equip the saints to do the work of ministry that Jesus has given to each of them.

3. **The Unity of the Church:** It is largely intrinsic and organic in that it is built around focusing on Jesus and His gifting of each one to do His desired work.

4. **Continuity in the Church's Ministry:** Focusing on Jesus as the leader and the local body's collective gifting brings continuity. The organic composition of that local body and Jesus' leadership form a stable foundation not found when building upon shifting philosophies of ministry due to a change in "senior pastors" that brings new emphases and new grace-gift mixes.

Such a view of strong visionary leadership with Jesus as the senior pastor is radically different from the CEO model that many American Christians indiscriminately have adopted from the American business community. By training pastors to be CEOs, we ironically end up training them to lead in exactly the same way as the "Gentiles" lead (Matt. 20:25/Mark 10:42). Such are the tragic payoffs of a defective theology of leadership.

The amazing irony is that the American business community has been moving away from this type of top-down leadership for over a generation. They learned that it just does not work. Listen to this astonishing quote from *Servant Leadership: A Journey into the Nature of Legitimate Power and Greatness*, written by Robert K. Greenleaf, a retired AT&T executive, in 1977:

> A new moral principle is emerging, which holds that the only authority deserving one's allegiance is that which is freely and knowingly granted by the led to the leader in response to, and in proportion to, the clearly evident servant stature of the leader. Those who choose to follow this principle will not casually accept the authority of existing institutions. *Rather, they will freely respond to individuals who are chosen as leaders because they are proven and trusted as servants.* To the extent that this principle prevails in the future, the only truly viable institutions will be those that are predominantly servant led.[9]

Drawing heavily from his Christian roots (as a Quaker), Robert Greenleaf also founded The Greenleaf Center for Servant-Leadership in Indianapolis a few years before his death in 1990. He started an amazing movement that has impacted the American business community. Perhaps it can now cross back over into the community that spawned it: the organic, sustainable church of Jesus Christ.

Chapter Thirteen

BIBLICAL LEADERSHIP IN THE SUSTAINABLE CHURCH

....

"Brothers, we are not professionals. We pastors are being killed by the professionalizing of the pastoral ministry. The mentality of the professional is not the mentality of the prophet. It is not the mentality of the slave of Christ. Professionalism has nothing to do with the essence and heart of the Christian ministry. The more professional we long to be, the more spiritual death we will leave in our wake. For there is no professional childlikeness (Matt. 18:3); there is no professional tenderheartedness (Eph. 4:32); there is no professional panting after God (Ps. 42:1)."

–John Piper[1]

"PASTORS" ARE ACTUALLY "ELDERS" OR "OVERSEERS"

Few biblical terms have been as distorted and redefined throughout church history as the term "pastor." By our contemporary usage, one would be hard-pressed to connect the New Testament's definition and description of pastoral ministry with those that we call "pastors" today. Therefore, let's take a brief look at the central New Testament passages that reveal the three terms that give the three perspectives of the leaders of local churches:

- The primary term for local church leaders is *"elders"* (literally "older men"). This term has a long heritage throughout Israel's history and the word even appears seven times in Acts for "the elders of the people" of Israel. There are 16 New Testament references to *Christian elders of local churches* (10 in Acts and 6 in the epistles).

- A secondary term for local church leaders is *"overseers."* As a noun it is used once for "the office of overseer" (1 Tim. 3:1), four times for the overseers of local churches (Acts 20:28; Phil. 1:1; 1 Tim. 3:2; and Titus 1:7), and once for Jesus as *"the Overseer of your souls"* (1 Pet. 2:25). It appears once as a verb in a textually debated passage in 1 Peter 5:2 where the Apostle Peter exhorts elders to be *"exercising oversight"* for the flock of God among you.

- The other secondary leadership term is *"shepherd"* and *it only appears as a verb to exhort church leaders to shepherd the flock of God* in Acts 20:28 and 1 Peter 5:2. It is quite noteworthy that the noun *"shepherd"* ("pastor") is never applied to local church leaders, but *only* to Jesus in the New Testament.

  o "[20]Now may the God of peace who brought again from the dead our Lord Jesus, *the great Shepherd of the sheep*, by the blood of the eternal covenant, [21]equip you with everything good that you may do his will." (Heb. 13:20-21a ESV)

  o "For you were continually straying like sheep, but now you have returned to *the Shepherd and Overseer of your souls."* (1 Pet. 2:25; my translation) o [the Apostle Peter to elders] "And when *the Chief Shepherd appears*, you [under-shepherds] will receive the unfading crown of glory." (1 Pet. 5:4)

The conclusion demanded from the New Testament terms and the usage of these terms for our local church leaders is that we have isolated and glorified the wrong term—"pastor"—for a local church leader. In so doing we have lost two very important things: 1) the plurality of the group of elders who are to overseer as under-shepherds and 2) our focus on the only one the New Testament calls "*the shepherd*": Jesus.

THE BIBLICAL DUTIES OF ELDERS

Elders are needed in every church. This is true even if your elders are new believers, like those Paul and Barnabas chose in the four pioneer-evangelism church-plants on their first missionary journey in Galatia:[2]

- "[21]And after they had preached the gospel to that city [Derbe] and had made many disciples, they returned to Lystra and to Iconium and to Antioch, [22]strengthening the souls of the disciples, encouraging them to continue in the faith, and saying, 'Through many tribulations we must enter the kingdom of God.' [23]*And when they had appointed elders for them in every church*, having prayed with fasting, they commended them to the Lord in whom they had believed." (Acts 14:21-23)

- [Paul to Titus after their pioneer evangelism church-plants on the island of Crete] "For this reason I left you in Crete, that you might set in order what remains *and appoint elders in every city as I directed you*." (Titus 1:5)

The elders' task is to shepherd the flock of God:

- [to the Ephesian *elders*, Acts 20:17] "Be on guard for your-selves and for all the flock, *among whom* the Holy Spirit has made you *overseers, to shepherd the church of God* which He [Jesus] purchased with His own blood." (Acts 20:28)

- "¹Therefore, I exhort the elders *among you*, as your fellow elder and witness of the sufferings of Messiah, and a par-taker also of the glory that is to be revealed, ²*shepherd the flock of God among you...*" (1 Pet. 5:1-2a)

- "¹⁴Is anyone among you sick? *Let him call for the elders of the church*, and let them pray over him, anointing him with oil in the name of the Lord; ¹⁵and the prayer offered in faith will restore the one who is sick, and the Lord will raise him up, and if he has committed sins, they will be forgiven him." (James 5:14-15)

The elders' role is to shepherd God's church which Jesus purchased with His own blood. But the elders' posture is as *under-shepherds who are among God's people, not over them.* This language is very intentional in emphasizing the relational con-nectedness of under-shepherds to the flock, not an "otherness" and certainly not an "overness". This is why Peter underscores the relational dynamic when he says, "nor yet as lording over those allotted to your charge, but proving to be examples to the flock." (1 Pet. 5:3)

Elders are accountable to Jesus, the Chief Shepherd:

- "Obey your leaders and submit to them, *for they keep watch over your souls, as those who will give an account.* Let them do this with joy and not with grief, for this would be unprofitable for you." (Heb. 13:17)

- "*¹Therefore, I exhort the elders among you... ²shepherd the flock of God among you... exercising oversight* not under compulsion, but voluntarily, according to the will of God; and not for sordid gain, but with eagerness; *³nor yet as lording over those allotted to your charge*, but proving to be examples to the flock. *⁴And when the Chief Shepherd appears, you will receive the unfading crown of glory.*" (1 Pet. 5:1-4)

Jesus as the Chief Shepherd has delegated some of the on-site shepherding (or pastoring) of His local flocks to local elders. They shepherd at His behest and on His behalf. They will give an account to Messiah Jesus as to how they have cared for *His flock* and He will reward them if they have shepherded faithfully.

ELDERS MUST BE BIBLICALLY QUALIFIED:[3]

	1 TIMOTHY 3:1-7	TITUS 1:5-9
Regarding God	• not a recent convert	• holy
Regarding Self	• sober-minded • self-controlled • not a drunkard • not a lover of money	• disciplined • self-controlled • not a drunkard • not greedy for gain • not quick-tempered • a lover of good

	1 TIMOTHY 3:1-7	TITUS 1:5-9
Regarding Family	• husband of one wife[4] • manages own household well • children are in dignified submission	• husband of one wife • children are believers • children are not debauched or insubordinate
Regarding the Word	• able to teach	• hold firm to the trustworthy Word as taught so that he may be able to give instruction in sound doctrine and also to rebuke those who contradict it
Regarding Community	• not violent, but gentle • not quarrelsome • hospitable • above reproach • respectable • well thought of by outsiders	• not violent • not arrogant • hospitable • above reproach (2 times) • upright

It is absolutely essential to see that one's home and local community are the two crucial proving grounds for a person's character and qualification to be an elder. If there is distrust and lack of respect in the community, one should not be an under-shepherd of God's people. If one has failed to create a godly environment and to lead in his own household, then why would you consider this person qualified to help lead the household of God? As Dr. Howard Hendricks, one of my beloved professors used to say in one of his memorable accents, "If it doesn't work at home, don't export it!"

Additionally, the emphasis of these 20+ qualifications is primarily on one's character and history, not on one's skills or gifts. In fact, the only skills that are mentioned are "*able to teach*" and "*able to exhort in sound doctrine and to refute those who contradict.*" Being able to teach the Bible is a key part of the elders' shepherding of God's flock. *Notice that all elders are to shepherd and, therefore, should be able to feed the flock, i.e., teach.* But, as we will soon see, teaching has been artificially separated in church history from the biblical role *of all elders* and has been designated for only *"vocational" elders.* This creates a bizarre distortion in language between the overlapping terms *elders* and *overseers* who are to shepherd (Acts 20:17-32 and 1 Pet. 5:1-4). Over the centuries the church wrongly designated the term "shepherd" or "pastor" only for the "vocational" elders, distorting the New Testament's teaching about the shepherding by all elders.

SHOULD ELDERS BE PAID?

The biblical answer in the New Testament is "Yes!" Why? Because of this biblical principle in the Old and New Testaments: when others minister *spiritual things* to us, we are honor-bound before the Lord to minister *material things* to them.[5] This is one reason why the priests and Levites shared in a portion of the temple offerings and sacrifices in Israel (e.g., Lev. 27:30-33; Num. 18:8-32; cf. Deut. 14:28-29). This principle continues in the New Testament era:

- "*[11]If we sowed spiritual things in you, is it too much if we should reap material things from you?* [12]If others share the right over you, do we not more? Nevertheless, we did not use this right, but we endure all things, that we may cause no hindrance to the gospel of Christ. [13]Do you not know that those who perform sacred services eat the food of the temple, and those who attend regularly to the altar have their share with the altar? *14So also the Lord directed those who proclaim the gospel to get their living from the gospel."* (1 Cor. 9:11-14)

- "And let the one who is taught the word share all good things with him who teaches." (Gal. 6:6)

- [regarding the collection among Messianic Gentiles for the impoverished Messianic Jews in Judea] "26For Macedonia and Achaia have been pleased to make a contribution for the poor among the saints in Jerusalem. 27Yes, they were pleased to do so, and they are indebted to them. *For if the Gentiles have shared in their spiritual things, they are indebted to minister to them also in material things."* (Rom. 15:26-27)

- *"17Let the elders who rule well be considered worthy of double honor, especially those who work hard in the word and teaching.* 18For the Scripture says, 'You shall not muzzle the ox while he is threshing,' [Deut. 25:4] and 'The laborer is worthy of his wages'" [Lev. 19:13]. (1 Tim. 5:17-18; translation is mine)

There are several essential things to grasp in these passages. First, *every elder* is to be "able to teach" (1 Tim. 3:2) and "holding fast the faithful word which is in accordance with the teaching, that he may be able both to exhort in sound doctrine and to refute those who contradict" (Titus 1:9). This means that all elders are to teach the Word of God and are worthy of having those who are taught "share all good things with him who teaches" (Gal. 6:6).

Secondly, in the 1 Timothy 5 passage, the term "honor" has a financial connotation throughout the chapter. It is first applied in verse 3 to "Honor widows who are widows indeed." In the following discussion in verses 4-8, the term "honor" means to care financially for widows by children and grandchildren, if she has them.[6] If not, then Paul gives some guidelines in verses 9-16 for widows to be qualified for the church's support.

Paul then continues the discussion of who is worthy of "honor"—financial support by the local church—in 5:17 when he begins to discuss the honoring of elders. Observe that Paul says in verse 17 that those elders who rule well are worthy of "double honor," "especially those who work hard in the word and teaching." This only makes sense if all of the elders were worthy of "single honor"—that is, some financial remuneration. Each of the elders must have gotten something from God's people because "nothing doubled is still nothing." In other words, *God's people were to give back material support for the spiritual teaching and shepherding that each of the elders gave them.* For elders to take time to care for the flock and to prepare to teach them in the assembly or "to exhort in sound doctrine and to refute those who contradict" in various settings, they would have had to take time away from their craft or their farming. To make up the financial shortfall, God's people were to honor them for the sacrifice of their lost income in order to "sow spiritual things" by letting them reap material things. These elders became essentially "bi-vocational" when they assumed the office of elder in their local congregation.

Being bi-vocational seems to be God's design for most elders when God's people assume their biblical responsibility of materially rewarding them. Sadly, this is no longer the norm in the Western church.

Those elders who were giving the vast majority of their time to "ruling well" and "working hard in the word and teaching" (1 Tim. 5:17) essentially had left their craft or their farming and were likely working full-time for God's people. The appropriate response of the flock was to make up the shortfall financially by doubling the single-honor financial remuneration that all of the elders normally received. Whether this was equivalent to a full-time salary that one could live on, we don't know. It may have still necessitated some form of bi-vocational work. However, the crucial point is that this increased financial giving by God's people was not something that was promised or expected on the front-end by the elder. Rather, it was a response by God's people on the back-end in light of the sacrificial labors by this elder. He had not entered a "profession" that led to candidating for and accepting a job with a local church. Rather, his hard work in the Scriptures and his leading the flock well in his own church had led to their organically shifting him from a bi-vocational status to essentially a vocational status with the fellowship.

Additionally, understanding that the pastorate was not viewed as a separate vocation requiring a seminary degree may help us make sense out of some of the elder qualifications and warnings to elders that relate to money. For example, Paul says that an elder is to be "free from the love of money" (1 Tim. 3:3) and that elders should "not be fond of sordid gain" (Titus 1:7). Peter exhorts the elders in like manner in 1 Peter 5:2 when he says "shepherd the flock of God among you, exercising oversight not under compulsion, but voluntarily, according to the will of God; and not for sordid gain, but with eagerness." These passages seem to acknowledge that aspiring elders can sometimes be inappropriately motivated by money. If an aspiring elder's heart is set on financial reaping from God's people instead of the spiritual sowing into God's flock, he is not qualified for the role.

The clear understanding this should lead us to regarding paying elders is this: *There was **not** a great dichotomy between elders in the New Testament who were paid and those who weren't paid.*

Why? Because *God's people were supposed to remunerate **all** of the elders for their sowing of spiritual things into the lives of Jesus' flock.*

There was absolutely no dichotomy between "lay elders" and "clergy elders". Additionally, there is no biblical distinction between "teaching elders" and "ruling elders." This is a later development in church history and an unbiblical one.[7] The distinction is negated by the fact that a qualification of *all elders* is that they are to teach and exhort in sound doctrine. This means that local churches need to be training and growing future elders who will be worthy of single honor, and some who may eventually serve in a such manner that they become worthy of double honor. Elders must be willing to become "bi-vocational." This is God's design for His under-shepherds who serve at the pleasure of Jesus, the Chief Shepherd.

AN EXAMPLE OF LIVING OUT THESE BIBLICAL PRINCIPLES

I encountered this issue with my fellow leaders in a church we planted as a team in Baltimore in July 1980. Marty and I were one of six founding couples. After three and a half months of forming a core group, we began to meet publically in mid-October in a public school where we rented the cafeteria for our assembly and some classrooms for the children. By Christmas time, our six-person leadership team got wind that our small congregation of about 30-40 folks wanted to give a special Christmas gift to the two of us leaders who were paid at that time. Some folks in our new congregation were thinking in the familiar categories of church tradition that it is the paid folks who are "the pastors" of the church. Because the other four of our leaders had jobs where they were well paid and could take time off work to help oversee and shepherd the congregation, they did not want to be remunerated. This helped fuel the flock's misunderstanding of the biblical principles undergirding our church's salary strategy.

Since the six of us met weekly as leaders, we promptly discussed this Christmas-gift-strategy before it came to fruition. My emphasis with our team was that all six of us were involved in leading and shepherding the flock and that it was inappropriate to single out two of us who happened to be salaried at the time. Wanting to avoid fostering an unbiblical hierarchy among the leaders, we decided as a team that if the congregation wanted to give a Christmas gift to us leaders, it would need to be to all six of us. Since our four brothers who had good-paying jobs did not feel comfortable receiving this kind of a Christmas gift from our small congregation, we decided that none of us would get a congregational Christmas gift. This was costly to our young family as we were expecting our second child on December 28th and had no health insurance. However, we felt that the principle that there is *no dichotomy* between elders who are paid and those who are not was an important principle to underscore in the life of our young church. While it made for a few less Christmas gifts for a couple of our families, it was well worth championing the principle of *no dichotomy.*

CONCLUSION: WHO IS THE PASTOR OF YOUR CHURCH?

Periodically I will do some teaching in one of the mega-churches of Southern California where I live. If I happen to mention that I spoke at such a church, invariably people will say, "Oh, isn't that Pastor X's church?" I will jokingly use the occasion to express the biblical perspective by saying, "No. It's Jesus' church, but Pastor X is there." You can imagine the nervous laughs and sometimes guilty looks that I get in response to my statement. But the point needs to be made: No church is "Pastor X's church."

1. Don't fire the Chief Shepherd.

I hope you are persuaded that Messiah Jesus is your church's pastor and that He is "the Shepherd and Overseer of your souls" (1 Pet. 2:25). Of course, as "the great Shepherd of the sheep" (Heb. 13:20) and as the "Chief Shepherd (Pastor)" (1 Pet. 5:4), Jesus has delegated some of the on-site shepherding of His local flocks to local shepherds. But these local elders are directly accountable to the Chief Shepherd as to how they are caring for *His* flock. Elders "keep watch over your souls, as those who will give an account" (Heb. 13:17) regarding "those allotted to your charge" (1 Pet. 5:3).

Picture a shepherd with several flocks of sheep who continually overseers his under-shepherds of each flock. This is what Jesus has been designated to do ever since the Father fired Israel's shepherds and made the Davidic Messiah the One and Only Shepherd of God's people (Ezekiel 34). Jesus' explanation that "I am the Good Shepherd" in John 10:1-18 is the fulfillment of the long-awaited Messianic Shepherd. He has been doing His shepherding ever since. *So why would we want to displace the climactic Messianic Shepherd with Pastor X?*

2. Don't miss the biblical plurality of under-shepherds.

There is marvelous safety and a much healthier, balanced spiritual diet when there is a plurality of overseers (who meet the Bible's elder qualifications) shepherding a local church under the clear headship of Jesus, the Chief Shepherd. The relationships between these under-shepherds should model an interpersonal, family dynamic that the local body can learn from and imitate. This is why the Apostle Peter said to the elders, "nor yet as lording it over those allotted to your charge, *but proving to be examples to the flock*" (1 Pet. 5:3). Given that social learning theorists assert that we learn over 95% of all we will ever know by imitating models, this is the most economical and powerful way we learn. Having a plurality of mature leaders as readily accessible models is an educational bonanza for learning what the Christian life is like.

A plurality of elders also brings balance and multiple personal models with different personalities and different grace-gifts. The local body is not just being imprinted by one personality with one history and one set of grace-gifts. Rather, as they share in the teaching of the flock, they bring spiritual variety and balance to the teaching of God's Word. God's people need to experience this variety in order to have a healthy, balanced spiritual diet. Moreover, no one person can have 50 weeks of truth per year flowing through their soul. This invariably leads an overseer in a single-shepherd model to traffic in unlived truth. It also leads many overseers to start pulling the sermons of others off the Internet and *presenting them as their own work.* More importantly, God's people suffer by being taught by people who have not had the time or energy to internalize and apply God's Word to their own lives. Listeners can sense the teachers' lack of personal connection with God's truth and this negates the significance and relevance of what they were trying to teach.

3. Don't miss the sustainability of a biblical plurality of under-shepherds.

The New Testament teaches by both example and clearly stated principles that the most spiritually mature leaders who are biblically qualified to be elders are those who should be paid for their shepherding of the local flock. Since the majority of them were bi-vocation and likely had to cut back the hours they worked in their craft or their farming in order to give time to shepherding Jesus' flock, God's people were to respond by letting them reap material things for their sowing of spiritual things (1 Cor.

9:11). The biblical model also recognizes that some elders may give all their working time to the local flock, shifting organically from being bi-vocational to being vocational with God's people. The church should respond to this sort of elder by giving him "double honor" (1 Tim. 5:17).

One of the beauties of this organic biblical model is that this person's character is already known and proven to meet the biblical qualifications for an elder. Additionally, this person and his family are already well known and loved by the flock. The church is not bringing in a stranger who looks good on paper. His time of "candidating" is not a few days and two or three teaching times, but likely spans several months or years and in many different circumstances, as he and his family live in the midst of this local flock. This seems to be God's design for the choosing of "vocational shepherds" for His church.

Lastly, this model seems to be God's design for how churches all over the world and throughout church history can sustain quality leadership. Probably the vast majority of local churches throughout church history, especially in the two-thirds world (the non-Western world), have been sustained largely through bi-vocational leadership. This should not be viewed as defective or less-than. Rather, it is a sustainable model that does not devour a large percentage of a local church's weekly offering. By contrast, after two generations of financial prosperity, the typical American evangelical local church spends 70-90% of its budget on staffing and facilities. This would not have been sustainable for most churches throughout church history. Sadly, however, this model of large paid staffs and expensive facilities is seen as the desired standard for churches throughout the world. Churches with multiple bi-vocational overseers that meet in homes or rented facilities—what the church did for centuries—are seen as embarrassing or shameful. I would be so bold as to predict that this standard will likely change in America as the broader culture becomes increasingly antagonistic to the evangelical church and its beliefs. Coupled with a four-generation decline in percentage giving among evangelicals,[8] the model of large staffs and costly facilities will become clearly unsustainable. Perhaps we will have to rediscover a few things:

- A state-of-the-art building is a luxury, not a necessity for a local church.

- A biblical model of sustainable leadership is built around a plurality of under-shepherds, most of whom are bi-vocational.

- We must train and equip the saints more effectively and intensely in local churches so we can produce more mature believers and leaders.

Perhaps we will have to rediscover the model of the sustainable church that has been right before our eyes in God's Word the whole time.

Chapter Fourteen

HOW LEADERS CAN CULTIVATE THE SUSTAINABLE CHURCH

....

"One of the unintended consequences of contemporary church strategies that revolve around *performances, places, programs,* and *professionals* is that somewhere along the way *people* get left out of the picture. But according to Jesus, *people* are God's method for winning the world to himself. *People* who have been radically transformed by Jesus. *People* who are not sidelined to sit in a chair on Sundays while they watch professionals take care of ministry for them. *People* equipped on Sundays to participate in ministry every day of the week. *People* who are fit and free to do precisely what Jesus did and what Jesus told us to do. Make disciples."

–David Platt[1]

ELDERS LOSING SIGHT OF *PEOPLE*

The widespread appearance of theater seats in the buildings where local churches meet is a telltale sign of the evangelical church's increased focus on performances, places, programs and professionals. People come to see a performance of sorts that both entertains and inspires. Skilled professionals are expected to run a polished and skillfully enacted program. In larger churches there may even be "a stage-manager" who keeps "the performers" on schedule and keeps "the performance" running smoothly. Skits, videos and music flow through a state-of-the-art sound system, keeping the performance moving along at an entertaining clip.[2]

We have believed the popular idiom, "If we build it, they will come." Because this mantra has been implicitly adopted as a crucial part of the formula for church growth in North America, it is tragically understandable why so many evangelical churches spend 70-90% of their annual budget on staffing and facilities. They are following the popular paradigm that you need *professionals* to create *programs* with great *performances* at nice *places* if you want others to come and see. But what about the *people?* A whole generation was overlooked and under-challenged to grow as disciples of Jesus. We focused on polishing *the forms* and missed fulfilling *the biblical functions* in the process.

THE ULTIMATE PEOPLE-FOCUS: MOBILIZE THE SAINTS IN THE WORK OF THE MINISTRY

Jesus gave some of the grace-gifts to members of His body so they could help all the other members find their role on the team:

> [11]And He gave some as apostles, and some as prophets, and some as evangelists, and some as pastors-teachers, [12]for the equipping of the saints for the work of service [or "ministry"], to the building up of the body of Christ; [13]until we all attain to the unity of the faith, and of the knowledge of the Son of God, to a mature person, to the measure of the stature which belongs to the fullness of Messiah. (Eph. 4:11-12; my translation)

Some local church elders may have one or more of the four equipping gifts, likely the fourth one (apostles, prophets, evangelists, and *pastor-teachers*). However, the equipping of the saints was never intended to be dependent upon the elders of a local church having any or all of these grace-gifts. The dispensing of these mobilizing gifts is spread throughout the body of Christ and does not necessitate that those who have them must or should be elders. Rather, those who are elders are those who meet the biblical qualifications to be a shepherd. Since an elder must be "able to teach" it is more likely that he has one of the five grace-gifts associated with the Word of God (teaching, *pastor-teacher*, exhortation, word of knowledge or word of wisdom) and he may also have the gift of leading. Again, note that *pastor-teacher* is also one of the equipping gifts and it would be helpful if at least one of the elders had this gift.

The crucial question is this: Why should the elders' focus be on mobilizing all the saints in their local flock to join in the work of service (ministry)? The most obvious answer comes from Ephesians 4:13 where Paul indicates *the goal* for the equipping of the saints in 4:11-12: "until *we all arrive* at the unity of the faith and the full knowledge of the Son of God, to a mature person, to the measure of the stature of the fullness of Messiah."[3]

The goal of all the saints discovering their gifting and their role in the body of Christ *is so that we together arrive at unity and maturity in Christ.* As we discussed in Chapters Ten and Eleven, this is "body discipleship" where the body of Christ builds itself up in love as all of the parts fulfill their roles. Paul expands on this as he gives *the purpose* for the equipping (Eph. 4:14-16):

> [14]so that we may no longer be children, tossed here and there by waves, and blown around by every wind of doctrine, by the cunning of men, by their craftiness in deceitful scheming; [15]but speaking the truth in love, we are to grow up in every way into Him, Who is the Head, into Messiah, [16]*from Whom the whole body, being joined and knitted together by every joint which is supplied, according to the proper working of each*

individual part, causes the growth of the body for the building up of itself in love.[4]

Messiah Jesus has two purposes in giving grace-gifts to His body "for the building up of itself in love":

First, His *quantitative* purpose: Jesus wants to bring about the fulfillment of God's promised blessing, through the seed of Abraham, to all the world's people-groups (Gen.12:3; Gal. 3:8). Paul makes it clear that the indwelling Holy Spirit is the specific Abrahamic blessing and it is imparted to all people-groups *through Messiah Jesus*:

> [13]Messiah redeemed us from the curse of the Law, having become a curse for us—for it is written, 'CURSED IS EVERYONE WHO HANGS ON A TREE'—[14]*in order that in Messiah Jesus the blessing of Abraham might come to the peoples, so that we might receive the promise of the Spirit through faith.*" (Gal. 3:13-14, my translation and emphasis; see also Acts 2:33 for the exalted Jesus' outpouring of the *promised* Holy Spirit).

This is why Messiah Jesus focuses His newly received resurrection authority on the universal imparting of this blessing in "the Great Commission" (Matt. 28:16-20). Jesus' disciples— aptly named "the body of Christ"—are His present means of imparting the Abrahamic blessing through our making disciples of Him among the rest of the world's people-groups. In particular, the apostles understood the specific fulfillment of the commission as the evangelizing of unreached peoples and the gathering of them into local churches, as the Book of Acts faithfully records. Therefore, local-to-global church-planting should be a central focus of every church until Jesus returns.

Our commission to focus on creating communities of Jesus' disciples all over the world also anticipates God's desired end of the present phase of human history:

"⁹After these things I looked, and behold, a great multitude, which no one could count, *from every nation and all tribes and peoples and tongues,* standing before the throne and before the Lamb, clothed in white robes, and palm branches were in their hands; ¹⁰and they cry out with a loud voice, saying, 'Salvation to our God who sits on the throne, and to the Lamb.'" (Rev. 7:9-10; my emphasis)

It seems that the Father's goal for human history is to have a ransomed people from every tribe, tongue and people-group of the world arrayed around His throne (cf. Rev. 5:9-10; 15:2-4). Why such a goal for history? The best answer I can give is that *this goal* will bring God the greatest glory. If this were not so, then He would have chosen another end of history to satisfy His just demands. Additionally, God the Father's righteous choice of a universal kingdom represented by every people-group on planet earth fulfills God's creation purpose for humanity. What was lost after the creation with the first Adam will be regained and fulfilled under the second and greater Adam, Messiah Jesus (Heb. 2:5-8). This global goal compels Messiah's international harvest and focuses the Holy Spirit's anointing of Messiah's people to empower them to fulfill this mission (e.g., Acts 1:8). This is *the quantitative purpose* for Messiah Jesus' giving of grace-gifts to His people in Ephesians 4:11-16.

Secondly, His *qualitative* building-up purpose: Messiah Jesus wants to bring about the spiritual maturing of His people into His likeness—Christlikeness—as we are fulfilling the global mission He has given us. The shepherding of God's people by the under-shepherds of local churches is not an end in and of itself. Rather, it is a crucial means to the end of fulfilling the climactic historical mission that Messiah Jesus has given to us, while simultaneously beautifying and maturing his bride in the process.

How can elders think that they are rightly shepherding God's people when there is no meaningful emphasis on grace-gifts? Our grace-gifts are the fruit of the ascended Messiah's triumph over the spirit-world (Eph. 4:7-10) and the means that the Holy Spirit uses in our service of Him (Eph. 4:11-16). By not focusing on the saints discovering and growing in the use of their grace-gifts, elders thwart both *the historical mission* that Jesus has given us and also *the spiritual means of maturing us* that He has given us. Tragically, we do this without batting an eye.

Elders, please listen to me: Our task as under-shepherds is much more focused than we think. It is also easier than we think because *it is not all about our leadership.* It is about the Chief Shepherd's leadership expressed in and through the empowering of His people to fulfill the commission He gave us. When we align with Lead Pastor Jesus and mobilize His people to discover, use and grow in the use of their grace-gifts, the saints' ministries take on a life of their own. It is not about us and our vision for the church. It is about under-shepherds knowing and implementing the Chief Shepherd's vision for our local church. That vision is broadly the same all over the world, even allowing for certain local distinctives within the parameters of the global mission.

FIVE WAYS LEADERS CULTIVATE THE SUSTAINABLE CHURCH

1. Require each church member to discover, develop and use their grace-gifts in their ministry.

Notice that we are talking about "their ministry," not "our ministry" as a church leader. They are not serving us as we lead in our ministry; we are there as servant leaders to support *them* in their ministry to serve Jesus. This starts with helping them discover what grace-gifts Messiah Jesus has given them. In the two church-plants where I served, we required each aspiring member to go through our Grace-Gifts Seminar (available for free at www.sustainablehchurch.org). It was usually scheduled on a Saturday morning a couple of weeks after they completed our "Discovery Class," where they learned about being a member of "the ministry team." This is the seminar's basic outline:

First, we'll answer seven crucial questions about grace-gifts:

1. *What* is a "grace-gift" or "spiritual gift"?

2. Who *distributes* the grace-gifts?

3. Who *gets* the grace-gifts?

4. *When* are the gifts given?

5. What is *the basis* for the giving of the gifts?

6. *Why* are the gifts given—for what purpose?

7. *Why* do people with the same gift have *different effects* in ministry?

Second, we'll go over the process of discovering your grace-gifts.

Third, we'll look at the list of biblical passages mentioning grace-gifts and go over the summaries of each grace-gift.

Lastly, we'll fill out the "Grace-Gifts Inventory" and share our results with a group of 4-5 other grace-gifted saints.

The goal of this seminar is to educate and motivate each of these saints about their grace-gifts. I have never failed to see God's people get excited about discovering their role in the ministry and mission that Jesus has given us. For many believers this is a spiritual turning point. Once they discover their gifting and begin to develop and use their gifts, their ownership and engagement in the work of God is never the same.

2. Resource each saint regularly, in light of their grace-gifts, to bolster them in *their* ministries.

In our church-plants we created a spreadsheet with each member's name and their corresponding grace-gifts. We had a couple of amazing women with the gift of administrations who oversaw this aspect of ministry with an astonishing competency and faithfulness. They made the information available to each of us as elders so that we could be knowledgeable of each member's grace-gifts. This made the regular resourcing and encouraging of our people about their gifting much easier.

What did we do to regularly encourage our people about their gifts and their ministries? We did several things. First, we continued to supply training in different areas that would aid in the development of certain grace-gifts. Second, we continually put reading materials into their hands that related to their ministries and gifting. I copied countless articles from Christian magazines and biblical journals over the years and gave them to saints who were gifted in related areas. I bought and gave or lent books to folks to stimulate them in the use of their gifts. Third, we were always looking for conferences to send our people to that would help them grow in their gifting. For example, we sent dozens of our members to Larry Crabb's training seminars in the area of counseling. We also bought the seminar videos and made them available to those who couldn't go to the seminars. Over the years this type of training made a huge difference in our body's ability to deal with life's hurts and pains. Finally, we tried to connect those who had newly-discovered grace-gifts with those who had more maturity in Christ and more developed grace-gifts in similar areas for mentoring relationships.

One amazing example is a woman who really thrived in counseling and became a leader in that area in our church. We connected her with a Christian psychologist in the area who became her mentor for the next 30 years. As a result of this mentoring relationship, the lives of thousands of people were positively impacted for Jesus Christ.

3. Focus on the saints using their grace-gifts in *every* weekly assembly by briefly interviewing different members of the body regarding their gifting or by having a sharing time where saints speak about using their gifts in *their* ministries.

Whatever a church regularly gives time and space to in its weekly assembly reveals that church's core values over time. People will intuit over the weeks and months that something is valuable because it gets consistent air time and other things are not important because they are essentially ignored. If 95% of the church service is taken up with singing and preaching, then the saints will gather that these are the two most important things in the Christian life. However, if mobilizing the body of Christ to do the work of ministry is important (and it is) then we should be talking about and showcasing it when we gather. Is it any wonder that only 10-20% of Jesus' disciples know what their grace-gifts are in light of sitting for years with hands folded in laps "while they watch professionals take care of ministry for them"[5]? How can we chastise God's people for their passivity when they are accurately responding to the meta-message we give them every Sunday?

4. Do leadership development for all who want it.

Contrary to popular opinion and to the emphasis of the last few generations, the best place to develop future leaders for every facet of the life of the local church is *in the life of the local church.* Having trained men and women in a local church setting in two different church-plants, I have seen their amazing growth and the development of their grace-gifts and biblical knowledge as adult learners. The beauty of adult learners is that "they know what they don't know." They are very hungry to learn. They see the symbiotic relationship between their doing and learning. It is no exaggeration to say that many of these folks trained in their local church were more adept at teaching God's Word after 3-4 years of training than the vast majority of M.Div. graduates. Additionally, they were in relationship with those whom they served and with whom they partnered in ministry. This added the integrative relational piece to their learning that is almost totally absent in our individualistic academic settings.

It is immensely important that we do robust leadership development in our local churches. This training is where many of our future leaders will be developed. It becomes the life-blood for future elders, church-planters and missionaries. If more training is desired beyond the local church's capacity, then partnering with Christian colleges, universities and seminaries is always available. We helped to finance the education of many of our future missionaries through partnering with evangelical schools.

5. Recognize and distinguish between cultural forms and biblical functions.

The following diagram seeks to help define the difference between the forms or structures for ministry that we use and the biblical functions that the forms are supposed to be accomplishing. When all is said and done, we should absolutize the biblical functions and be flexible and open to changing the cultural forms of ministry in order to fulfill those biblical functions.

SEPARATING *"FUNCTIONS"* FROM *"FORMS"* IN THE LIFE OF THE CHURCH

FUNCTIONS ⟵ VERSUS ⟶ FORMS

FUNCTIONS	FORMS
• Non-negotiable, timeless (absolute)	• Negotiable, temporal (relative)
• Directives to accomplish church's goal	• Methods for accomplishing church's functions
• Based on God's Word	• Based on cultural needs
• That every church must be actively pursuing	• That every church is free to choose
Function (definition): A non-negotiable, timeless directive for accomplishing the church's goal based on God's Word that every church must be actively pursuing.	**Form (definition):** A negotiable, temporal method for accomplishing the church's functions based on cultural needs that every church is free to choose.

Of course, the mistake that many churches and many Christians make is absolutizing the cultural forms and thereby making it unthinkable that we would ever do certain things in any other manner than the way we have done them for many years. For example, one of the best forms for accomplishing the biblical function of evangelism was to have a "revival"—i.e., a week of evangelistic meetings—in the spring and in the fall. When America was composed primarily of rural communities, a spring meeting followed the end of crop planting and a fall meeting followed the end of harvest. These cultural forms fit the rural farming lifestyle and calendar, plus folks were excited about going to the revival meetings since the church was the social center of most rural communities. It was a meaningful form that helped to achieve the biblical function.

However, several generations later in post-rural America, it makes little sense to put a sign in front of local churches advertising "Spring Revival" or "Fall Revival". There is no rural farming life-style and calendar in most communities and local churches are generally no longer the social hub. If we've absolutized the form and don't have the courage to evaluate its effectiveness for the biblical function, we will persist in using the form and feel like we're being faithful. While there is value in holding on to a sense of history as God's people, it should never be an end in and of itself. We are not accountable to the Lord for preserving history, but for fulfilling the biblical functions that He has given us.

This is why we used the above diagram to teach our people during their membership class to recognize the purpose of our cultural forms in accomplishing the biblical functions. Occasionally a saint would come up to one of the other elders or to me and say something like, "Walt, I don't think this particular form is accomplishing the corresponding biblical function." They would explain the weakness of the form and then suggest a different cultural form to fulfill the desired biblical function. I would find myself saying the vast majority of the time, "Thank you so much! I think you are absolutely right. Let's try the new form that you suggested and see if it works better in fulfilling the biblical function." By treating the saints as adults and helping to equip them for *their* ministries, *they* became a part of the change process, rather than just sheep doing only what the shepherd told them to do. This gave them a much greater sense of ownership and competency in *their* ministries.

A FINAL WORD

The opening of Ephesians used to strike me as containing a bit of hyperbole. In 1:3, Paul writes, "Blessed be the God and Father of our Lord Jesus the Messiah, *who has blessed us with every spiritual blessing in the heavenly places in Messiah.*"[6] Over the years, however, as I have studied more about Messiah Jesus' work in giving us grace-gifts, I've seen that there is really no hyperbole at all.

From this astonishing statement about all the spiritual blessings in heavenly places that we have in Messiah Jesus, Paul then adds an equally astonishing statement about how God has given the church mind-boggling observers of her spiritual blessings:

> [8]To me, the very least of all saints, this grace was given to preach to the Gentiles the unfathomable riches of the Messiah, [9]and to bring to light what is the administration of the mystery which for ages has been hidden in God, who created all things; [10]*in order that the manifold wisdom of God might now be made known through the church to the rulers and the authorities in the heavenly places.*[7] (Eph. 3:8-10)

As God's people we have been given all spiritual blessings in the heavenly places and the rulers and authorities in the heavenly places—likely evil spirit beings in this context—are observing us to see how God will manifest His previously hidden, multifaceted wisdom. We are being watched by millions and millions of spirit beings all throughout space who both oppose and support God's kingdom. But that's not the end of the astonishing statements about our blessings in Messiah Jesus. Paul adds how those blessings were achieved through the ascension of Messiah Jesus:

> [7]*But to each one of us grace was given according to the measure of Messiah's gift.* [8]Therefore, it says, '*WHEN HE ASCENDED ON HIGH, HE LED CAPTIVE A HOST OF CAPTIVES, AND HE GAVE GIFTS TO MEN.*' [9]Now this expression, 'He ascended,' what does it mean except that He also had descended into the lower parts, that is the earth? [10]He who descended is Himself also He who ascended far above the heavens, that He might fill all things.[8] (Eph. 4:7-10)

Messiah Jesus conquered the malevolent spirits through His death, burial, resurrection and, especially, His ascension. This is when He took His messianic spiritual warfare spoils—powerful grace-gifts—and began dispensing them to His people. Because of these grace-gifts, He "has blessed us with every spiritual blessing in the heavenly places" (Eph. 1:3). *It is therefore through the church's use of these powerful grace-gifts that we manifest God's kingdom plan and purposes to millions and millions of defeated spirit beings in the heavenly places* (Eph. 3:8-10).[9]

Can you grasp the cosmic significance of ignoring the spiritual firepower that individual Christians have? Can you grasp the cosmic foolishness of building the church's ministry around a handful of leaders and their grace-gifts rather than around all the saints and their grace-gifts? This is why churches built around performances, places, programs and professionals are ultimately weak, pale manifestations of spiritual power and authority. It's like countering an artillery barrage with a water pistol. In the midst of spiritual warfare, it is not a sustainable church.

Instead, we should be building the church's ministry around all the saints and their powerful grace-gifts. Messiah Jesus' incarnation, life, death resurrection and ascension have empowered us with the spiritual armament to win the battle of both earth and the heavenly places. This demands that we wake up and smell the flaming arrows and respond in obedience to God's equipping of us. However, He has delegated the hands-on discovery of our spiritual equipment to those gifted to equip the saints for the work of ministry (Eph. 4:11-12) and to the leaders of local churches to foster this work. This leads to the sustainable church.

Will you choose to be *a functional part* of the grace-gifted church? If you are a leader, will you choose to foster the equipping of the saints in the body of Christ? I pray that you will. It's a vital task. It is God's grace-filled design for local churches to flourish in spite of adversarial social contexts, difficult economic climates and the natural inertia of a fallen world. It is God's plan for His people to be active, alive and sustainable in the world, serving and bearing witness to His glory as the beloved bride, the organic body and the eternally sustainable church of Messiah Jesus.

For more information about *Sustainable Church*
and to access the free Grace-Gifts Seminar and Inventory,
please visit *www.sustainablechurch.org*

Appendix #1

THE ISSUE OF CESSATIONISM

....

THE CESSATIONIST UNDERSTANDING OF TEMPORARY AND PERMANENT GRACE-GIFTS

Temporary (nine gifts)

- **Foundational:** Apostleship, Prophesying, Word of Knowledge, Word of Wisdom

- **Confirmatory:** Miracles, Healing, Tongues, Interpreting of Tongues and Discerning of spirits

Permanent (ten gifts)

Faith, Teaching, Helps/Serving, Mercy, Evangelizing, Pastor-Teacher, Leading/Ruling, Administrations, Giving, and Exhortation

If we could turn back the calendar thirty years, the vast majority of American evangelicals would say that this diagram accurately expresses its beliefs about grace-gifts. They would say that they believe in *cessationism* and therefore are *cessationists* because they believe that nine of the 19 grace gifts *ceased* with the death of the apostles early in the second century AD. I was one of these evangelicals for twenty years. Two of my three graduate theological degrees are from wonderful schools that are strongly *cessationist*. I believed what I was taught about cessationism and passed it on rather passionately to those whom I taught from 1970 until about 1990.

However, somewhere along the way, I began to look afresh at the issue of grace-gifts and ended up changing my mind. I was not alone. The face of evangelicalism has changed on this issue over the last 30 years. As I survey my faculty colleagues and graduate theological students, the vast majority of them could be labeled as conservative evangelicals who believe that all of the gifts are still given today. This is a phenomenal change over the last generation in the United States. Ironically, we are now where most Christians in other parts of the world have been for some time.[1]

I first got excited about grace-gifts when I was a *cessationist* and was only looking at ten gifts. By the way, it was a lot easier to write an inventory for discovering your grace-gifts when I was only dealing with 10 rather than 19 gifts. My point is that I have emphasized the importance of equipping the saints by helping them to discover their grace-gifts whether I believed that there were 10 or 19 of them. *Your commitment* to equipping the saints should not be dependent upon how many gifts you think are functioning today. That should be a non-issue in terms of your emphasis upon God's people discovering, developing and using their grace-gifts.

My personal path that led to me changing my mind was not based on any experience that I had speaking in tongues, having dreams and visions, or performing miracles or healings. I have experienced none of those things. Rather, my path was through studying the Bible. Three biblical things persuaded me that I had been wrong in my original view of grace-gifts.[2] First, and most persuasive to me, was the simple thought that if 47% of the grace-gifts ended (nine out of 19), the New Testament should make a fairly big deal out of it in more than one passage. However, there is *not one* New Testament passage that states that these gifts have ceased. Rather, we use what I call "multi-level" theological arguments to try and prove that nine of these gifts are no longer given.

Secondly, the five main passages that are used to support *cessationism*—Acts 2:43 and 5:12; 2 Corinthians 12:12; Ephesians 2:19-20; and Hebrews 2:1-4—no longer persuaded me. Paul writes this in 2 Corinthians 12:12: "*The signs of a true apostle* were performed among you with all perseverance, *by signs and wonders and miracles*" (my emphasis). Hebrews 2:3b-4 makes a similar point: "After it was first spoken through the Lord, it was confirmed to us by those who heard, *God also testifying with them, both by signs and wonders and by various miracles and by gifts of the Holy Spirit* according to His own will" (my emphasis). Acts 2:43 and 5:12 both confirm that *many signs and wonders* were taking place through the hands of the apostles. Cessationists argue from these four passages that the purpose of the miraculous gifts of the Holy Spirit—especially miracles and healings—was *to confirm the apostles and their message.* With the death of the apostles came the end of the need to confirm their apostolic work of founding the church. Hence, these temporary, foundational, miraculous gifts ceased. This is the type of "multi-level" argument that I mentioned earlier.

It is absolutely true that the signs and wonders performed by the apostles did help to confirm their spiritual authority (2 Cor. 12:12 and Heb. 2:3-4). However, one cannot *assume* that this confirmation was *the only purpose* for these signs and wonders. It may be only one part—and a very important one—of a larger whole. A quick survey of Acts reveals that other purposes for the signs and wonders were to bring great joy to those who see God's liberating power (Acts 8:6-8) and to provide evangelistic persuasion to believe in Jesus (Acts 9:32-35).

Moreover, we cannot also *assume* that the signs and wonders were to be performed *only by the apostles*. Acts specifically states that there are those beyond the apostolic circle who performed them: Barnabas in Acts 14:3 and 15:12, Stephen in Acts 6:8 and Philip in Acts 8:6, 13. In light of this, it seems far more likely that when the author of Hebrews says, "it was confirmed to us *by those who heard*" (Heb 2:3b; my emphasis), that his generic description—*those who heard*—was intended to be broader than Paul and the twelve to be accurate. If this is so, then a purpose of the signs and wonders that *encompasses* the apostolic confirmation is *to confirm the spiritual power of the gospel message*. I would suggest that this continues to be an ongoing purpose for the signs and wonders' gifts in many parts of the world.

Perhaps a good cessationist response to this would be, "Okay, the phrase *those who heard* describes not just the apostles, but *the apostolic generation*. Signs and wonders ceased with the passing of that generation when the written Scripture replaced their eyewitness testimony." Again, this is going well beyond what the biblical text says. For example, the point of Hebrews 2:1-4 is to exhort the readers/listeners to pay closer attention to the word of the new covenant that they have heard (v. 1). The explanatory undergirding of v. 1's exhortation in vv. 2-4 is one of the many examples in Hebrews of *an argument from a lesser to a greater*. Usually the author argues from the old covenant to the new, as he does here. His point is that if the lesser old covenant had a strict judgment for disobedience, imagine how much stricter the judgment will be under the greater new covenant. Note the basic structure of the paragraph with my annotations:

(2:1) The Exhortation to Listen Carefully

[1]For this reason we must pay much closer attention to what we have heard, so that we do not drift away *from it.*

(2:2-4) The Explanatory Undergirding of this Exhortation: The Argument From the Lesser Old Covenant to the Greater New Covenant

[2]For if the word spoken through angels proved unalterable, and every transgression and disobedience received a just penalty, [3]how will we escape if we neglect so great a salvation?

The Greater Revealing of the New Covenant

(1st Stage) After it was at the first spoken through the Lord,

(2nd Stage) it was confirmed to us by those who heard, [4]God also testifying with them, both by signs and wonders and by various miracles and by gifts of the Holy Spirit according to His own will.

To bolster his point in Hebrews 2:3b-4, the author describes the surpassing nature of the new covenant revelation compared to the old. The old was revealed through angels (v. 2a),[3] but the new was first revealed through the Lord's speaking (v. 3b). It was then confirmed by those who heard, "*God also testifying with them,* both by signs and wonder and by various miracles and by gifts of the Holy Spirit according to His own will" (vv. 3c-4; my emphasis). Again, note that all of this language is in the service of strengthening *the exhortation* "to pay closer attention to what we have heard" (v. 1). Also notice that one reason for the superiority of the new covenant is God's *more direct involvement* in its revealing. He spoke it first *through the Lord Jesus* and then also testified with those who confirmed it.

With all of this as background, we are now ready to ask the key interpretive question of the passage in light of its usage by cessationists: Would we expect that an aspect or implication of this explanatory undergirding of the greater new covenant in vv. 2-4 is to express *the temporary nature* of that which confirmed it, i.e., the signs and wonders, various miracles, and *some, but not all*, of the gifts of the Holy Spirit?

Let me answer this crucial question with two points. First, Hebrews 2:2-4 is neither the time nor the place to make this point, even if it were true. Second, if this were part of the meaning of this paragraph, then it would actually weaken, not strengthen, the author's support for his exhortation. The author of Hebrews states that the new covenant revelation began through Jesus' words and was confirmed by those who heard His words, but there is no hint of a limitation or terminus for those confirmations. To argue an important theological point in the absence of any corresponding implications in the text is not persuasive. One first has to assume a multi-level theological process that goes well beyond the implications of this passage's meaning.

While the first two issues I developed with cessationism were relatively easy to work through, my third and final biblical issue was not. It dealt with Paul's statement in Ephesians 2:19-22 about apostles and prophets:

> [19]So then you are no longer strangers and aliens, but you are fellow citizens with the saints, and are of God's household, [20]having been built on the foundation of *the apostles and prophets*, Christ Jesus Himself being the corner *stone*, [21]in whom the whole building, being fitted together, is growing into a holy temple in the Lord, [22]in whom you also are being built together into a dwelling of God in the Spirit (my emphasis).

Particularly vexing to me was the fact that *the apostles and [N. T.] prophets* in v. 20 seemed to be a part of the foundation of the church. Does it mean that these two groups of Spirit-gifted individuals did their foundational work and then disappeared from the church? If this is so, it seems to argue quite convincingly for *at least some cessationism.*[4] It was also confusing to me to think that *prophecy/prophets* ceased when Paul spilled a lot of ink proving the superiority of *prophecy over tongues* when the church gathers for her assembly (1 Cor. 14:1-40). This seems unnecessary if *both* of these grace-gifts were going to cease 40 years after Paul's letter.

So, how did I work through this issue and interpret Ephesians 2:19-22 in a sound, biblical manner? There were three parts to my reasoning. First, it was clear that *the apostles and prophets* of Ephesians 2:20 had a unique, unrepeatable role in founding the church and speaking, writing and authorizing the inerrant words of the New Testament. They were a unique group. I lean toward seeing them as two groups—*apostles and prophets*—rather than as one group, *apostle-prophets,* as Wayne Grudem does.[5] Second, I saw through my study that the topic in Ephesians 2-3 is the creation of the household of God (2:19) out of the Jews and Gentiles who believe in Jesus as the Messiah. In particular, previously this mystery of Christ "was not made known to the sons of men, as it has now been revealed to His holy *apostles and prophets* in the Spirit" (Eph. 3:5; my emphasis). The *apostles and prophets* were the specific ones who clarified "that the Gentiles are fellow heirs and fellow members of the body, and fellow partakers of the promise in Christ Jesus through the gospel" (Eph. 3:6).

Lastly, Grudem draws the conclusion that this passage does *not* describe "the character of *all who had the gift of prophecy* in the New Testament churches." He explains:

> I see no convincing evidence that it describes all who prophesied in the early church. Rather, the context clearly indicates a very limited group of prophets who were (a) part of the

very foundation of the church, (b) closely connected with the apostles, and (c) recipients of the revelation from God that the Gentiles were equal members with Jews in the church (3:5)... we are still left with a picture of a very small and unique group of people who provide this foundation for the church universal.[6]

I agreed with this reasoning and concluded that cessationists were theologizing far beyond what Ephesians 2:19-22 actually says. As with my previous points of dissonance with cessationism, I found that its appeal to a preexisting multi-level theological argument was necessary to fill in the gaps of what the biblical text did *not* say. I was persuaded by my study of these biblical issues to cease being a cessationist.

A NOTE ABOUT THE TERM "LEADERS" IN THE NEW TESTAMENT

....

MESSIAH JESUS IS THE SINGULAR LEADER AND CHIEF SHEPHERD OF GOD'S PEOPLE

All other spiritual leadership roles in the New Testament are *derived from* Messiah Jesus and *delegated by* Messiah Jesus to His under-shepherds. As I mentioned in the beginning of Chapter Thirteen, *the noun "shepherd"* (or "pastor;" Greek, ποιμήν) is only used as a title for Jesus.

- "²⁰Now may the God of peace who brought again from the dead our Lord Jesus, *the great Shepherd of the sheep*, by the blood of the eternal covenant, ²¹equip you with everything good that you may do his will." (Heb. 13:20-21a ESV)

- "For you were continually straying like sheep, but now you have returned to *the Shepherd and Overseer of your souls*." (1 Pet. 2:25; my translation)

- [the Apostle Peter to elders] "And when *the Chief Shepherd* appears, you [under-shepherds] will receive the unfading crown of glory." (1 Pet. 5:4)

This is because Jesus fills the office of *God the Father's only designated shepherd of His people* after God fires the shepherds of Israel (Ezek. 34, especially verses 23-24). This is why Messiah Jesus announces in John 10:11 that He is that designated shepherd: "*I am the good* shepherd; the good shepherd lays down His life for the sheep." See also John 10:14-16.

Another way to approach this data is to see that the three terms associated with local church leaders in the New Testament are derived from this description of Messiah Jesus:

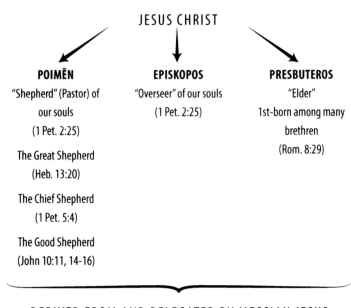

JESUS CHRIST

POIMĒN	EPISKOPOS	PRESBUTEROS
"Shepherd" (Pastor) of our souls (1 Pet. 2:25)	"Overseer" of our souls (1 Pet. 2:25)	"Elder" 1st-born among many brethren (Rom. 8:29)
The Great Shepherd (Heb. 13:20)		
The Chief Shepherd (1 Pet. 5:4)		
The Good Shepherd (John 10:11, 14-16)		

DERIVED FROM AND DELEGATED BY MESSIAH JESUS

THE UNDER SHEPHERDS

TO SHEPHERD/PASTOR   OVERSEER   ELDER

TO SHEPHERD/PASTOR	OVERSEER	ELDER
Acts 20:17-35	**1 Timothy 3:1-7**	**1 Peter 5:1-4**
"And from Miletus he [Paul] sent to Ephesus and called to him *the elders [presbuteroi] of the church.*" (v. 17) "Be on guard for yourselves and for all the flock, among which the Holy Spirit has made you *overseers [episkopoi], to shepherd [poimainō]* the church of God which He purchased with His own blood." (v. 28)	"It is a trustworthy statement: if any man aspires to the office of *overseer [episkopos]*, it is a fine work he desires to do. An overseer, then, must be...." (v. 1-2a)	"Therefore, I exhort the *elders [presbuteroi]* among you, as your fellow elder and witness of the sufferings of Christ, and a partaker of the glory that is to be revealed. *Shepherd [poimainō]* the flock of God among you, *exercising oversight [episkopeō]* not under compulsion, but voluntarily, according to the will of God; and not for sordid gain, but with eagerness; nor yet as lording it over those allotted to your charge, but proving to be examples to the flock. And when the Chief Shepherd, appears, you will receive the unfading crown of glory."
	Philippians 1:1	
	"Paul and Timothy, bond-servants of Christ Jesus, to all the saints in Christ Jesus who are in Philippi, including *the overseers [episkopoi]* and deacons.;"	
Titus 1:5-9		
"For this reason I left you in Crete, that you might set in order what remains, and appoint *elders [presbuteroi]* in every city as I directed you. ..For the *overseer [episkopos]* must be..." (vv. 5, 7a)		

Those who fill delegated under-shepherd roles among God's people are to imitate Jesus' example by being "servant-leaders" as He is:

- [42]And calling them to Himself, Jesus said to them, "You know that those who are recognized as rulers of the

Gentiles *lord it over them*; and their great men exercise authority over them. *[43]But it is not so among you, but whoever wishes to become great among you shall be your servant; [44]and whoever wishes to be first among you shall be slave of all. [45]For even the Son of Man did not come to be served, but to serve, and give His life a ransom for many.*" (Mark 10:42-45; parallels Matt. 20:20-28)

- [1]Therefore, I exhort the elders among you, as your fellow elder and witness of the sufferings of Christ, and a partaker also of the glory that is to be revealed, [2]shepherd the flock of God among you, exercising oversight not under compulsion, but voluntarily, according to the will of God; and not for sordid gain, but with eagerness; *[3]nor yet as lording it over those allotted to your charge, but proving to be examples to the flock.* [4]And when the Chief Shepherd appears, you will receive the unfading crown of glory. (1 Pet. 5:1-4)

The words for "leaders/leadership" in the New Testament are:

1. ἡγουμένους - "leaders"- (in Heb. 13:7, 17, 24; cf. Acts 15:22-23a)

   o "Remember *those who led you*, who spoke the word of God to you; and considering the result of their conduct, imitate their faith." (Heb. 13:7)

   o "Obey your *leaders*, and submit to them; for they keep watch over your souls, as those who will give an account. Let them do this with joy and not with grief, for this would be unprofitable for you." (Heb. 13:17)

   o "Greet all of your *leaders* and all the saints. Those from Italy greet you." (Heb. 13:24) o "Then it seemed good to the apostles and elders, with the whole church, to choose men from among them to send to Antioch with Paul and Barnabas—Judas called Barsabbas, and Silas, *leading men* among the brethren, and they sent this letter by them…" (Acts 15:22-23a)

o **Comment:** The three Hebrews 13 usages are referring to local church elders and the Acts 15 usage is used more broadly to describe those with some respected status among the believers. In the middle of the three Hebrews 13 usages (13:7, 17 and 24) is the reminder that Messiah Jesus is He whom the God of peace "brought up from the dead [and is] *the great Shepherd of the sheep through the blood of the eternal covenant, even Jesus our Lord"* (Heb. 13:20).

2. ἐπισκοπέω – "to exercise oversight" (of elders in 1 Peter 5:2)

   " ²shepherd the flock of God among you, *exercising oversight* not under compulsion, but voluntarily, according to the will of God; and not for sordid gain, but with eagerness;

   ἐπίσκοπος – "overseer(s)" (Acts 20:28; Phil. 1:1; 1 Tim. 3:2; Titus 1:7; 1 Pet. 2:25, of Jesus)

   o The first two references are to *the elders/overseers in Ephesus and Philippi*, respectively.

   o The references in 1 Timothy and Titus are introducing the biblical qualifications for overseers: "*The overseer*, then must be…."

o The 1 Peter 2:25 reference refers to Messiah Jesus: "but now you have returned to *the Shepherd and Overseer of your souls"* (1 Pet. 2:25b).

ἐπισκοπή – "office of an overseer" (1 Tim. 3:1)

o "It is a trustworthy statement: if any man aspires to *the office of overseer,* it is a fine work he desires to do." This is the only usage of this term in the New Testament that refers to the role of overseers as an office.

o **Comment:** These three terms all refer to the ministry of elders or overseers and reveal that these leaders are a delegated work by the chief overseer, Messiah Jesus (1 Pet. 2:25).

3. προισταμένους – "those who have charge over you" (1 Thess. 5:12)

o The difficulty with interpreting this term is that it was also used in Greek outside of the Bible to refer to patrons or benefactors *"who protect and care for you,"* as opposed only to those who have a delegated authority to lead and direct you. We see a bit of this "softer" sense of the term in 1 Timothy 3:4-5 where Paul speaks of the qualifications of an overseer regarding his own household: "⁴He must *manage* his own household well, with all dignity keeping his children submissive, ⁵for if someone does not know how *to manage* his own household, how will he take care of the church of God?" Note one's household is the training ground for being able to *"take care of"* God's family. This means to be able to "be concerned about, care for, or give aid." A similar "softer context" is in the list of grace-gifts in Romans 12:8 where this term is translated as "*the one who leads*" with zeal, yet is surrounded by the grace-gifts of those who exhort, contribute and do acts of mercy.

o   For a bit of context, note what Paul says in 1 Thessalonians 5:12-13: "[12]We ask of you, brothers, to respect those who labor among you and *are over you in the Lord* and admonish you, [13]and to esteem them very highly in love because of their work. Be at peace among yourselves." (ESV) This context tips the balance toward those who have the authority to lead God's people—i.e., elders/overseers—because they also have the authority *and responsibility* to teach or admonish God's people (e.g., "able to teach" in 1 Tim. 3:2). However, given the two possible meanings of the word we are investigating, it is not just a cold, stiff authority that elders are to exert, but also an authority that expresses care and concern for God's flock. That care and concern should first be manifested with one's own family before it is ever exported to the family of God (1 Tim. 3:4-5).

προεστῶτες – "who rule" (of elders in 1 Tim. 5:17 "who rule well")

o   This is actually from the same root word as the previous term we just discussed. This is the perfect active participle form of the verb προΐστημι. Paul's full statement in 1 Timothy 5:17 is this: "Let the elders who rule well be considered worthy of double honor, especially those who labor in *preaching* [likely "evangelism"] and *teaching* [what we call "preaching"]. You can see that we have gummed up the biblical terminology in referring to when the elders teach God's people.

However, Paul's point is clear in this passage. Those elders/overseers who regularly give large amounts of extra time to the work of the church are worthy of double the remuneration of typical elders. Again, their labors should express a care and concern in their communication to both unbelievers and to God's people, not just a sense of cold authority over others.

The Grace-Gift of Leadership in the New Testament

προιστάμενος – "the one who leads or gives aid" (Rom. 12:8)

o This word has the same root word in Greek as the previous two words: προΐστημι. Again, note the two possible meanings of the word. Given the other usages of the various forms of this word, this grace-gift in Paul's list in Romans 12:8 likely refers to "the one who leads." However, as in the other usages, to the original Greek readers this term would have a softening sense that partook of the sense of "giving aid." As we see in Jesus, the ultimate leader of leaders, there should be a servanthood aspect to one's leading of God's people that gives them aid and comfort as one expresses this gifting. Our model is our humble King of Kings, not a multi-national corporation CEO.

The Unusual Term that Jesus uses in Matthew 23:10

καθηγηταί – "leaders" in Matthew 23:10 NASV; "masters" in KJV; "instructors" in ESV; "teacher" in NIV/Net Bible;

καθηγητής – "teacher, mentor, guide, master, leader, one who shows the way (spiritually or intellectually?)" (in Matt. 23:10 of Jesus)

o Note well the difficulty in translating this term in Matthew 23:10 and the broad diversity in the various translations. This is a very rare and difficult term to translate and only occurs in this one verse in the New Testament.

The Context of Matthew 23:8-10 and Jesus' Final Rebuke of the Pharisees on Tuesday of Passion Week

Most of Matthew 23 is given to Jesus' confrontation with the Pharisees during His final visit to the Temple two days before His arrest. In Matthew 23:1-12, Jesus is exposing the Pharisees' actions that reveal their underlying desire to be noticed by people. He will also pronounce His final seven messianic woes upon them in 23:13-36. But first, he reveals how the Pharisees love places of honor at banquets and in the synagogues and respectful greetings in the market places (23:6-7). Jesus then gives a series of three titles that the Pharisees expected, but that are inappropriate for God's people to use (23:8-10). He then reiterates His paradigm for His leaders in 23:11-12: "[11]But the greatest among you shall be your servant. [12]And whoever exalts himself shall be humbled; and whoever humbles himself shall be exalted."

The Three Inappropriate Titles for Leaders of God's People in Matthew 23:8-10:

- [8]But do not be called *"Rabbi"*; for One is your Teacher, and you are all brothers.

- [9]And do not call anyone on earth *"your father"*; for One is your Father, He who is in heaven.

- [10]And do not be called *"leaders"* (or "guides"); for one is your Leader (or Guide), the Messiah."

Observations:

1. "Rabbi" and "father" are singular as titles in vv. 8-9, but the "leaders" or "guides" are plural in v. 10.

2. The plural title in v. 10a contrasts with the singular title of "the Messiah" in v. 10b.

3. Jesus' use of "the Messiah" in v. 10b is very unusual in Matthew. [1]

4. One would not expect a redundancy with v. 8 ("teacher") in v. 10 ("leaders" or "guides"). Surely Jesus is getting at another aspect of His authority that is usurped with the different title in v. 10a.

5. If "rabbi" in v. 8 is focusing on the teaching aspect of that title, then perhaps the title in v. 10 is focusing on the leadership or guidance of one like *"a tutor, mentor, or spiritual guide."*

6. If #5 is accurate, then the title in v. 10 may be addressing "more discipleship-like" relationships.

7. This is the conclusion of Bruce W. Winter in his excellent article, "The Messiah as the Tutor: The Meaning of καθηγητής in Matthew 23:10."[2] After discussing the use of the term καθηγητής in an ancient document dated AD 70-90 (*P. Oxy.* 2190), Winter reaches this conclusion in the last paragraph of his article:

> The term should therefore be regarded as a "functional" one, describing a relationship with a student

without in any way defining the level, or nature, of the education in which private instruction was given.[21] This accords well with its occurrence in Matthew 23:10. In verse 8 the relationship between Jesus, the Messiah, and his disciples brooks no intermediary Christian rabbis or schools. He is the διδάσκαλος [teacher], and they are all brothers—presumably from one generation to the next. This highly personalized relationship is even further defined in terms of a student to his καθηγητής, where Jesus, the Messiah, alone is to be *the* tutor.

8. The application of this understanding of a term like *"tutor, mentor, or spiritual guide"* is to be very careful that we do not give a spiritual title or the spiritual authority to another believer that rightfully belongs to our Messiah. He is to be our tutor, mentor and spiritual guide. Any help we get from fellow believers is exactly that: *from a fellow believer*. We are not their "disciple" nor are they our spiritual guide. That spiritual leadership role belongs solely and uniquely to Messiah Jesus. May God keep us from usurping or replacing His role.

ENDNOTES

....

Chapter One

1. See Frank Viola, *Pagan Christianity? Exploring the Roots of Our Church Practices* (BarnaBooks, 2008) for a pulse-quickening study of the source of most of our church practices like the sermon, the pastor, the order of worship, church buildings, Christian education, ministers of music, tithing and clergy salaries, etc. Viola's consistent point is that much (most?) of what we do in our churches is more informed by our (pagan) traditions than by the Bible. This book has been accused of being a bit overstated at points. Nevertheless, Viola's criticisms of many of our present practices are valid and warrant thoughtful investigation and consideration.

2. James Davison Hunter, *To Change the World: The Irony, Tragedy, and Possibility of Christianity in the Late Modern World* (New York: Oxford Press, 2010), 12; his emphasis.

3. Ibid., 17.

4. "Faithful Presence," An Interview with James Davison Hunter by Christopher Benson, *Christianity Today* (May 2010): 36.

Chapter Two

1. This quote is credited to Dr. Richard C. Halverson, chaplain to the U.S. Senate, for a speech before the General Assembly of the Presbyterian Church in 1984.

2. The specific passages are Romans 12:3-8; 1 Corinthians 12:12-31; Ephesians 1:22-23; 2:16; 4:1-16; 5:23, 30; and Colossians 1:18, 24; 2:19; 3:15.

3. See also 1 Corinthians 12:27; Ephesians 4:4; and Colossians 3:15.

4. See also Romans 12:4-5; 1 Corinthians 12:4-7; and Colossians 2:19.

5. "Survey Describes the Spiritual Gifts That Christians Say They Have," (The Barna Group, Feb. 9, 2009): <www.barna.org/barna-update/faith-spirituality/211-survey-describes-the-spiritual-gifts-that-christians-say-they-have>

6. Quoted in William McRae, *The Dynamics of Spiritual Gifts* (Grand Rapids: Zondervan, 1976), 11.

Chapter Three

1. There are at least three major interpretations of "when the perfect comes" in 1 Corinthians 13:10. The first view sees "the perfect" as the coming of the New Testament canon, i.e., the recognition of the biblical books of the N.T. as we know them. This view argues that certain grace gifts like prophecy, tongues and knowledge (13:8) ceased when the canon came. This view is called "cessationism" and generally pictures nine of the 19 gifts as *ceasing* because they were foundational and confirmatory gifts for the apostolic generation (see Acts 2:43 and 5:12; 2 Corinthians 12:12; Ephesians 2:19-20; and Hebrews 2:1-4). The contextual difficulty with this view in 1 Corinthians 13 is that the "now/then" language of 13:12 pictures a far more complete change—seeing face-to-face, knowing fully, and being fully known—than the N.T. canon brought. The second and third interpretations fit this "now/then" context much better. The second view sees "when the perfect comes" as the completion of the church and this present age at the return of Messiah Jesus. Such a framing of the Corinthians' use of their grace-gifts is *a continuation* of Paul's language at the beginning of the letter in 1 Cor. 1:4-9, especially v. 7: "so that you are not lacking in any spiritual gifts, as you wait for *the revealing of our Lord Jesus Christ*" (ESV; emphasis is mine). This interpretation also fits very nicely with Paul's use of the various maturing illustrations in this section (13:9-12). I hold this view because it seems to be more biblically supported. The third interpretation overlaps with the second in some ways, but sees "when the perfect comes" as the new heavens and the new earth of the eternal state (Revelation 21-22). Your eschatology (doctrine of the end times) may well determine whether you are drawn to the second or third interpretation. For a fuller discussion, see *Appendix #1*.

2. "Grace gifts" is the more accurate New Testament term rather than "spiritual gifts." See chapter 8 for a fuller discussion of the various grace gifts mentioned in this section.

3. Yes, this is an *unapologetic* advertisement for the excellent education available at my school.

4. I am especially familiar with and impressed by Crown Ministries, but there are several other outstanding Christian organizations.

5. Several years ago I had a graduate theological student with over $60,000 in credit card debt.

6. For a fuller discussion of New Covenant giving, see Walt Russell, *Generous Loving, Generous Giving: A Biblical Perspective on Giving* (Reclaimed Publishing, 2013; available at *Amazon.com*).

Chapter Four

1. "Experiencing God's Presents," *Christianity Today* (August 2003); accessed at http://www.christianitytoday.com/ct/2003/august/25.55 html

2. See Greg Ogden, *Unfinished Business: Returning the Ministry to the People of God* (Grand Rapids: Zondervan, 1990, 2003) Chapter 3, "Unveiling Our Institutional Mind-Set," for an interesting development of the history of terms like *laity* and *clergy*.

3. *Disciple* is used 238 times in the Gospels, especially in Matthew (74 times) and John (81 times). *Disciples* is also the most common name for Jesus' followers in Acts (29 times). After Acts, the term *disciples* is not used again in the New Testament. We'll discuss this more in Chapter Ten. The term *saints* occurs only four times in Acts. 53 of the 62 N.T. usages of *saints* are in Paul's letters (40 times) and Revelation (13 times).

4. For a marvelous exposition of Ephesians 4:1-6 and 4:7-10, see John R. W. Stott, *The Message of Ephesians* (The Bible Speaks Today; Downers Grove, Ill.: InterVarsity Press, 1979), 145-59.

Chapter Five

1. "Inexplicably, many commentators mix gift and office, yet they are not confused in the NT. *Certainly, there is nothing in the present context about an office.*" (Harold W. Hoehner, *Ephesians: An Exegetical Commentary* [Grand Rapids: Baker Academic, 2002], 539-40; my emphasis). This quote is preceded by six distinctions between "spiritual gift" and "office" and this statement, "Interestingly, the term 'office' is never used in the NT in connection with the gifts" (439). The discussion of Ephesians 4:7-16 is clearly about the grace-gifts that Christ gave (v. 7).

2. See Hoehner, *Ephesians*, for the explanation of the majority view of "one person with a combination of two gifts" (543). The sense is essentially "teachers who are pastors" (544).

3. For an excellent discussion of the issue of the continuation or ceasing of these gifts, see Wayne A. Grudem, general editor, *Are Miraculous Gifts for Today? Four Views* (Grand Rapids: Zondervan, 1996). The four views are cessationist, open but cautious, third wave, and Pentecostal/Charismatic. I personally know each of the four writers and they argue very graciously and well for their respective views. They also critique the three views that they do not hold. This book is a marvelous orientation to the issue, whether you are new to it or experienced.

4. See Hoehner, *Ephesians*, 547-51, for an in-depth discussion of the Greek grammar defending this understanding.

5. "Experiencing God's Presents," *Christianity Today* (August 2003): <http://www.christianitytoday.com/ct/2003/august/25.55 html>

Chapter Six

1. Slightly adapted from Greg Ogden, *Unfinished Business: Returning the Ministry to the People of God* (Grand Rapids: Zondervan, 1990, 2003), 76. This is a phenomenal book and I *highly* recommend it. It also has two very good chapters on equipping the saints.

2. *The Apostolic Fathers,* second edition, translated by J. B. Lightfoot and J. R. Harmer; edited and revised by Michael W. Holmes (Grand Rapids: Baker Book House, 1989), 112-113.

3. See the very stimulating book by my Biola colleague, Kenneth Berding, that strongly advocates that grace gifts are really *specific ministries* that God wants us to do. Ken's book is *What Are Spiritual Gifts? Rethinking the Conventional View* (Grand Rapids: Kregel Publications, 2006).

4. See Chapter 3, "A Short History of Christian Hospitality," in Christine D. Pohl, *Making Room: Recovering Hospitality as a Christian Tradition* (Grand Rapids: Eerdmans, 1999), 36-58.

Chapter Seven

1. Wayne Grudem defines *a spiritual gift* as "any ability that is empowered by the Holy Spirit and used in any ministry of the church." He then immediately explains his definition: "This broad definition includes both gifts that are related to natural abilities (such as teaching, showing mercy, or administration) and gifts that seem to be more 'miraculous' and less related to natural abilities (such as prophecy, healing, or distinguishing between spirits). The reason for this is that when Paul lists spiritual gifts (in Rom. 12:6-8; 1 Cor. 7:7; 12:8-10, 28; and Eph. 4:11) he includes both kinds of gifts." (*Systematic Theology: An Introduction to Biblical Doctrine* [Downers Grove, Ill.: InterVarsity Press, England and Zondervan, 1994, 2000] 1016.)

2. Paul uses a third Greek word that means *gift* (Greek, *doma*) in Ephesians 4:8. In this usage he is quoting Psalm 68:18 from the Septuagint (LXX), the Greek translation of the Old Testament, and using the term for *gift* that the LXX uses.

3. "Experiencing God's Presents," *Christianity Today* (August 2003): <http://www.christianitytoday.com/ct/2003/august/25.55 html>

4. For a very sobering but helpful book on this topic, see Gary L. McIntosh and Samuel D. Rima, *Overcoming the Dark Side of Leadership: How to Become an Effective Leader by Confronting Potential Failures,* revised edition (Grand Rapids: Baker Books, 1997, 2007).

5. I write these things about a Christian man who I have had the privilege of observing for over 40 years do these very things. He is my brother-in-law, Dr. Dennis George Rogers. I gratefully dedicate this description of how to develop the gift of faith to him.

6. For those who may want to study this culminating aspect of the ministry of the Holy Spirit in Luke-Acts, see my article, "The Anointing with the Holy Spirit in Luke-Acts," *Trinity Journal* 7 NS (Spring, 1986): 47-63.

Chapter Eight

1. *The First Epistle to the Corinthians*, 586. Balancing this a bit is Douglas Moo, *The Epistle to the Romans* (NICNT: Eerdmans, 1996) 764, who says of Rom 12:6-8: "These texts suggest that Paul, and presumably the early church generally, recognized a small number of well-defined and widely occurring gifts along with an indefinite number of other less-defined gifts, some of which may not have been manifest everywhere and some of which may have overlapped with others."

2. Harold W. Hoehner, *Ephesians: An Exegetical Commentary* (Grand Rapids: Baker Academic, 2002), 541; my emphasis.

3. Hoehner, *Ephesians*, 541-2; my emphasis.

4. Kenneth Cain Kinghorn, *Discovering Your Spiritual Gifts* (Grand Rapids: Zondervan, 1981), 11.

5. Hoehner, *Ephesians*, 542.

6. *The Epistle to the Romans*, 766-7.

7. According to Kinghorn, *Discovering Your Spiritual Gifts*, "Helps" is "a gift that leads to practical ministries to others, which relieve them, in turn, to perform still wider ministries" (12). "Serving" is "a task-oriented ministry that results in the supplying of material and temporal services to others in the Body of Christ, thereby freeing them to perform still other ministries" (13). While these seem to be very subtle and overly fine distinctions, they may be true.

8. See the very helpful article that clarifies that pastor-teacher is a *gift* not an office: Harold W. Hoehner, "Can a Woman be a Pastor-Teacher?" *Journal of the Evangelical Theological Society* (December 2007): 761-71.

9. See also Appendix #4: A Note about the Term "Leaders" in the New Testament.

10. See Fee, *The First Epistle to the Corinthians* (Grand Rapids: Eerdmans, 1987), 591-3, who agrees with the non-miraculous understanding of *word of wisdom*, but who sees *word of knowledge* as revelatory, or miraculous. He rightly sees the two gifts as parallel in some ways and very tightly tied to the Corinthians' fixation on knowledge and wisdom—especially the wisdom of the world (1 Corinthians 1:18-2:16).

11. Particularly concise and helpful is his discussion of *word of wisdom* and *word of knowledge* in his *Systematic Theology: An Introduction to Biblical Doctrine* (InterVarsity Press, England and Zondervan, 1994, 2000), 1080-82.

12. Sam Storms, *The Beginner's Guide to Spiritual Gifts* (Servant Publications, 2002), 42; my emphasis. While I have been persuaded of this under-standing of *a word of knowledge*, I am still vexed by Paul's statement in 1 Corinthians 14:6 that seems troublesome to both the miraculous and non-miraculous interpretations: "But now, brethren, if I come to you speaking in tongues, what will I profit you unless I speak to you either by way of revelation or *of knowledge* or of prophecy or of teaching?" (my emphasis). If *a word of knowledge* is a revelatory gift, then it is doubly redundant with "revelation" and "prophecy." However, if it is very similar to or is essentially "teaching," then we may also have a redundancy problem. This is why we must hold some of these interpretations with a loose hand.

13. See Grudem, *Systematic Theology*, 1082-3, for a brief discussion of this aspect.

14. C. S. Lewis, *The Screwtape Letters* (1942; HarperCollins paperback edition, 2001), 32.

15. One way to grow into a biblical worldview that includes the spirit world is to do some reading in this area. I suggest the following readings: C. S. Lewis, *The Screwtape Letters*; Charles H. Kraft, *Christianity with Power: Your Worldview and Your Experience of the Supernatural* (Vine Books/ Servant Publications, 1989); Paul G. Hiebert, "The Flaw of the Excluded Middle," *Missiology* 10 (1982) 35-47; reprinted in numerous readers like *Perspectives on the World Christian Movement: A Reader* (Pasadena, Calif.: William Carey Library Publishers, 2009); this is a classic article by a greatly respected evangelical missiologist about the need to enrich our Western worldview to biblical proportions by including the spirit world.

16. This tragic situation was also a function of this man's fellow elders' lack of life-on-life relationships with one another.

17. I am grateful to Grudem, *Systematic Theology*, 1062-3, for both the wording and the biblical examples in this sentence.

18. See Fee, *The First Epistle to the Corinthians*, 594, who sees this gift and the gift of *workings of mighty powers/miracles* in this manner: "each occurrence is a 'gift' in its own right."

19. See Grudem, *Systematic Theology*, 1069-80, for an excellent and biblically sound discussion of the grace-gifts of *tongues* and *interpreting tongues*. See also Del Tarr, *The Foolishness of God: A Linguist Looks at the Mystery of Tongues* (The Access Group, 2010), especially "Appendix #3—What 'Tongues' is Not," pages 405-14.

Chapter Nine

1. *19 Gifts of the Spirit* (Wheaton, Ill.: Victor Books, 1974), 7.

2. Zondervan Books, 1976, 110, with some modifications. The following discussion was originally based on his section, "The Process of Discovery," pages 111-19. Over the years, I have added my own insights.

3. This is Sam Storms' emphasis in *The Beginner's Guide to Spiritual Gifts* (Servant Publications, 2002), 159-65.

4. Parker J. Palmer, *The Courage to Teach: Exploring the Inner Landscape of a Teacher's Life* (Jossey-Bass Inc. Publishers, 1998), 30. I readily acknowledge that Palmer's perspective is very western, individualistic and "internal." Since most of the world's peoples still derive their identity from their defining *group*, they would be more external and group-oriented in determining *the desires of their group*. Moreover, they would not believe that one's true self is hidden within that person, but is visible to others like the fruit on a tree. Since this book is written primarily for readers with a western worldview, I have focused on our interest in internal desires rather than on group expectations.

5. Frank Tillapaugh and Rich Hurst, *Calling* (Dreamtime Publishing, 1997), 21; authors' emphasis.

Chapter Ten

1. James G. Samra, "A Biblical View of Discipleship," *Bibliotheca Sacra* 160 (April-June 2003), 231, footnote 37.

2. For example, see *The Master Plan of Evangelism* (Grand Rapids: Revell, 1963), Robert E. Coleman's iconic book advocating the Jesus model of discipleship that has sold over 3.5 million copies the last five decades.

3. Much of the research data in this section has come from the article on μαθητής (*mathêtês; disciple*) in the *Theological Dictionary of the New Testament*, Vol. IV, pages 415-460, edited by Gerhard Kittel; translated by Geoffrey W. Bromiley (10th edition; Grand Rapids: Eerdmans, 1977). This article is referred to in this chapter as "Kittel," with the appropriate page numbers.

4. *Renovation of the Heart: Putting on the Character of Christ* (Colorado Springs, Colo.: NavPress, 2002), 14; emphasis is mine.

5. The two exceptions are Acts 9:25 (likely referring to Paul's rabbinical disciples) and Acts 19:1 (referring to John the Baptist's disciples).

6. For example, see the popular book by Walter Hendrichsen, *Disciples Are Made Not Born: Making Disciples out of Christians* (Eerdmans, 1974). On a personal note, several years ago a friend and I were greeted by the leader of an influential discipleship ministry in Washington D.C. with these words: "I know you are Christians, but are you *disciples* of Jesus?" I had to bite my tongue to keep from explaining the interpretive error of his ways.

7. See Appendix #2, "A Note about the Term 'Leaders' in the New Testament," for a brief discussion of how difficult this word is to translate.

8. See Bruce W. Winter, "The Messiah as the Tutor: The meaning of καθηγητής in Matthew 23:10," *Tyndale Bulletin* 42 (1991), 152-57.

9. For a complete list of all of Paul's co-workers along with the additional terms "brother," "apostle," "servant," "partner," and "toiler," see E. E. Ellis, "Coworkers, Paul and His," Gerald F. Hawthorne, Ralph P. Martin, Daniel G. Reid, editors, *Dictionary of Paul and His Letters* (Downers Grove, Ill.: InterVarsity Press, 1993), 184.

10. James G. Samra, "A Biblical View of Discipleship," 230. Also see Samra's excellent scholarly book, *Being Conformed to Christ in Community: A Study of Maturity, Maturation and the Local Church in the Undisputed Pauline Epistles* (London: T & T Clark, 2008 paperback edition). Additionally, Jim Samra has written a shorter, more popular work about these concepts entitled, *The Gift of Church* (Grand Rapids: Zondervan, 2010).

Chapter Eleven

1. Dallas Willard, *Renovation of the Heart*,15.

2. For a fuller discussion of this issue, see my unpublished paper, "Confronting the Narcissistic Self: The Change in Personal Identity from the Bible to the 21st Century." It is available from the author upon request.

3. See Stephen Benko and John J. O'Rouke, *The Catacombs and the Colosseum* (Valley Forge, Penn: Judson Press, 1971), 154-57.

Chapter Twelve

1. Much of what follows is synthesized from a portion of my article, "40 Years of Church Growth: A View from the Theological Tower," *Journal of The American Society for Church Growth* 6 (1995), 17-41. See especially pages 26-33 for the complete text.

2. For example, by John N. Vaughan, "Trends among the World's Twenty Largest Churches," in *Church Growth: The State of the Art*, C. Peter Wagner, editor with Win Arn and Elmer Towns (Carol Stream, Ill.: Tyndale House Publishers, 1986), 131. See also Vaughan's *The World's Twenty Largest Churches* (Grand Rapids: Baker Books, 1984) and *The Large Church: A Twentieth Century Expression of the First Century Church* (Baker Books, 1985).

3. In one of the many recent articles about the burnout of American "clergy," G. Jeffrey MacDonald, "Congregations Gone Wild," *New York Times*, August 8, 2010, makes this observation: "As religion becomes a consumer experience, the clergy become more unhappy and unhealthy."

4. For a fuller discussion, see Walt Russell, "The Holy Spirit's Ministry in the Fourth Gospel," *Grace Theological Journal* 8 (1987), 227-39.

5. Charles Lee Feinberg, *The Prophecy of Ezekiel* (Chicago: Moody Press, 1969), 195. In Ezekiel 34 the focus is largely upon the political shepherds (kings) of Israel.

6. Note that Jesus the Messiah's concern as the Great Shepherd is for His disciples to gather the plentiful harvest of shepherdless sheep. The primary focus of this age in Matthew's Gospel is that the peoples of the world be discipled and shepherded *by Messiah Jesus* (e.g., Matt. 28:16-20).

7. In a very important messianic passage, Psalm 2:7-9, the psalmist speaks of Messiah's enthronement in the messianic office as God's Son (v. 7). He receives *the nations* as his coronation gift (v. 8) and He will *shepherd* them with a rod of iron (v. 9). The Apostle Paul asserts that this was fulfilled at Jesus' resurrection (Acts 13:30-33; Romans 1:1-5). The point is that even in the Old Testament, Messiah's shepherding role was seen to extend beyond Israel to the nations.

8. Andrew D. Clarke, *Serve the Community of the Church: Christians as Leaders and Ministers* (First-Century Christians in the Graeco-Roman World; Eerdmans, 2000), 249. Clarke does a brilliant job underscoring the servant-leader profile that Jesus' under-shepherds should have. See especially his conclusions on pages 249-52.

9. *Servant Leadership* (Paulist Press, 1977, 1991, 2002), 23-4; his emphasis.

Chapter Thirteen

1. *Brothers, We are NOT Professionals* (Nashville, Tenn: Broadman & Holman Publishers, 2002), 1-2.

2. While these new elders were new believers in Messiah Jesus, they were most certainly chronologically older in order to fulfill the meaning and intent of the term *elder*: "older man." Paul expresses the normative standard for elders in situations other than pioneer church-planting situations in 1 Timothy 3:6: "and not a new convert, lest he become conceited and fall into the condemnation incurred by the devil."

3. According to the language of *The English Standard Version*.

4. The four most common interpretations of "husband of one wife" are: The elder must be married; The elder cannot be a polygamist; The elder cannot have a second marriage: a widower cannot remarry and no divorce and remarriage; The elder should be a *"one-woman-man"*: i.e., exhibiting exemplary faithfulness to his wife in a culture where marital infidelity was common. This is the preferred interpretation and truest to the emphasis of the Greek phrase.

5. For a fuller discussion of biblical giving in both the Old and New Testaments, see my book, *Generous Loving, Generous Giving* (Fullerton, Calif.: Reclaimed Publishing, 2013; 102 pages), available on Amazon.com.

6. The term "honor" also has a financial connotation in the 5th of the Ten Commandments: "*Honor* your father and your mother, that your days may be prolonged in the land which the Lord your God gives you." (Exodus 20:12). We know this specifically by Jesus' rebuke of the Pharisees for their man-made tradition of "Corban" in Mark 7:8-13 where persons consecrated all of their assets to God. By this action, they could not fulfill the 5th commandment (7:10a) by financially "honoring"/helping their parents, "thus invalidating the Word of God by your tradition which you have handed down" (Mk 7:13a).

7. See Piper, *Brothers, We Are NOT Professionals*, for a multi-faceted appeal to avoid the vocational, professional mindset.

8. See Christian Smith, Michael Emerson and Patricia Snell, *Passing the Plate: Why American Christians Don't Give Away More Money* (New York: Oxford University Press, 2008).

Chapter Fourteen

1. David Platt, *Radical: Taking Back Your Faith from the American Dream* (Colorado Springs, Colo.: Multnomah Books, 2010), 90-91; emphasis is mine.

2. Not that the arts shouldn't have a significant place when God's people gather to worship. They should. But the use of the arts in worship is to help us to be more God-focused, not to be more self-focused and fulfill a demand to be entertained. The last thing we need is more encouragement to be self-focused.

3. My translation.

4. My translation.

5. Platt, *Radical: Taking Back Your Faith from the American Dream,* 90.

6. My translation and emphasis.

7. My translation and emphasis.

8. My translation and emphasis.

9. For a marvelous discussion of Messiah Jesus' conquest and defeat of the spirit world and His sharing of the spiritual spoils with His followers, see *God is a Warrior,* chapter 9, "Paul: The Warrior's Defeat of Principalities and Other Powers," by Tremper Longman III and Daniel G. Reid (Grand Rapids: Zondervan, 1995), pages 136-164.

Appendix #1

1. In 1996 Wayne Grudem noted that a group that is "gigantic in the evangelical world" and likely the majority position of evangelicals in the United States today is the "open, but cautious" position. See Wayne A. Grudem, general editor, *Are Miraculous Gifts for Today? Four Views* (Zondervan, 1996), 13. The intervening years since Grudem's observation have done nothing but reinforce the majority percentage of this group.

2. Again, I recommend Grudem's book, *Are Miraculous Gifts for Today? Four Views* for a much more sophisticated and extensive defense of *cessationism* and the alternative of the full continuation of all gifts. See especially Sam Storms' "The Ceasing of Cessationism," 185-206.

3. See Deuteronomy 33:2 for the initial reference to angelic presence being associated with Mount Sinai, and then the New Testament's mentioning of it in Acts 7:38, 53; Galatians 3:19; and, of course, Hebrews 2:2.

4. For example, Richard Gaffin, a cessationist, makes this point in *Are Miraculous Gifts for Today? Four Views,* 45. D. A. Carson, not a cessationist, says that the only *charisma* (grace-gift) that ceases is that of *apostleship,* defined "in the tightly defined sense" of the twelve and Paul who had personal contact with the resurrected Jesus (in *Showing the Spirit: A Theological Exposition of 1 Corinthians 12-14* [Grand Rapids: Baker Book House, 1987], 155-6).

5. See his more accessible book, *The Gift of Prophecy in the New Testament and Today* (Wheaton, Ill.: Crossway, 1988, 2000) and its more technical precursor, *The Gift of Prophecy in 1 Corinthians* (University Press of America, 1982).

6. Wayne Grudem, *Systematic Theology: An Introduction to Biblical Doctrine* (InterVarsity Press, England and Zondervan, 1994, 2000), 1051, footnote #4.

Appendix #2

1. R. T. France, *The Gospel of Matthew* (NICNT; Grand Rapids: Wm. B. Eerdmans, 2007), 864.

2. Bruce W. Winter, "The Messiah as the Tutor: The Meaning of καθηγητής in Matthew 23:10," *Tyndale Bulletin* 42 (1991), 152-157.

For more information about Walt Russell
or to contact him for speaking engagements,
please visit *www.sustainablechurch.org*

Many voices. One message.

Quoir is a boutique publishing company
with a single message: Christ is all.
Our books explore both His
cosmic nature and corporate expression.

For more information, please visit
www.quoir.com

CPSIA information can be obtained
at www.ICGtesting.com
Printed in the USA
FSOW01n0217090117
29381FS